Passion Gems

DAILY WISDOM ON THE
SUFFERING, CROSS, AND DEATH OF JESUS

DONALD H. CALLOWAY, MIC

with DAVID P. BUGAJSKI, MIC

Available from:
Marian Helpers Center
Stockbridge, MA 01263
Prayerline: 1-800-804-3823
Orderline: 1-800-462-7426
ShopMercy.org

Websites:
FatherCalloway.com
Marian.org
TheDivineMercy.org

Publication Date:
March 5, 2025

Imprimi Potest:
Very Rev. Chris Alar, MIC
Provincial Superior
The Blessed Virgin Mary, Mother of Mercy Province
Feast of Pope St. John Paul II
October 22, 2024

Nihil Obstat:
Robert A. Stackpole. STD
Censor Deputatus
October 22, 2024

ISBN: 978-1-59614-635-8
Library of Congress Control Number: 2024949844

Printed in the United States of America

MARIAN PRESS
STOCKBRIDGE   MA 01263

It is very good and holy to consider the
Passion of our Lord and to meditate on it,
for by this sacred path we reach union with
God. In this most holy school we learn
true wisdom, for it was there that
all the saints learned it.

— St. Paul of the Cross

INTRODUCTION

Jesus once told St. Faustina Kowalska, one of the greatest saints of modern times, the following:

> **There is more merit to one hour of meditation on My sorrowful Passion than there is to a whole year of flagellation that draws blood; the contemplation of My painful wounds is of great profit to you, and it brings Me great joy** (*Diary*, 369).

To modern man, penitential practices such as flagellation might seem outdated, but what Jesus is getting at is that meditation on His Passion is greater than any kind of external mortification or act of penance we can do. There's nothing wrong with mortifying oneself and practicing forms of penance, but ultimately it is the Passion of Jesus that obtains life for the soul and greatly increases our love for our dear Savior.

In *Passion Gems: Daily Wisdom on the Suffering, Cross, and Death of Jesus*, you will discover a treasure trove of quotes on the Passion of Jesus from Sacred Scripture, saints, popes, mystics, and revered laymen. For every day of the year you will be able to meditate and ponder a particular thought or theme regarding the loving Passion of Jesus. As Jesus said to St. Faustina, such meditation not only is of great merit and profit to us, but it also brings joy to the Heart of our Savior.

Part of the "Gem" series offered by Marian Press, *Passion Gems* was initiated by my confrère Br. David Bugajski, MIC. In *Passion Gems*, Br. David and I collaborated in gathering and arranging the quotes. We pray that you draw much merit and profit from reading the daily meditations. In these crazy and evil times in which we live, may you have peace and joy as you daily call to mind how much Jesus loves you and wants you to be with Him in Heaven.

Very Rev. Donald H. Calloway, MIC, STL
Vicar Provincial, Marian Fathers of the Immaculate Conception of the B.V.M., Blessed Virgin Mary, Mother of Mercy Province

JANUARY

January 1

Mary is also the one who obtained mercy in a particular
and exceptional way, as no other person has. At the same
time, still in an exceptional way, she made possible with
the sacrifice of her heart her own sharing in revealing
God's mercy. This sacrifice is intimately linked with the
cross of her Son, at the foot of which she was to stand on
Calvary. No one has experienced, to the same degree as
the Mother of the Crucified One, the mystery of the Cross,
the overwhelming encounter of divine transcendent justice
with love: that "kiss" given by mercy to justice.
— POPE ST. JOHN PAUL II

Holy Mary, Mother of God, pray for us!

January 2

In the Old Law, men doubted whether God loved them with a tender love; but after seeing him die on a Cross for us, how can we doubt of the tenderness and the ardent affection with which he loves us? Let us raise our eyes, and look at Jesus, the true Son of God, fastened with nails to a gibbet, and let us consider the intensity of the love which Jesus bears us.

— ST. ALPHONSUS LIGUORI

Heart of Jesus, generous to all who turn to You,
have mercy on us!

January 3

Live in such a way that all may know that you bear outwardly as well as inwardly the image of Christ crucified, the model of all gentleness and mercy.

— St. Paul of the Cross

Blessed be the name of Jesus!

January 4

God is love. In this the love of God was made manifest among us, that God sent his only-begotten Son into the world, so that we might live through him. In this is love, not that we loved God but that he loved us and sent his Son to be expiation for our sins.

— 1 John 4:8–10

Lord, have mercy. Christ, have mercy.

January 5

To take away a single sin, even venial in nature, a finite satisfaction is not really sufficient, even though it were lifelong, for it remains finite satisfaction while the offense is infinite. Hence, for satisfaction of an offense that is infinite in character, it would be necessary that God himself made such satisfaction. Only such satisfaction could suffice to repair the offense and injury against the divine justice. Of course, for such satisfaction it would not have been required that Jesus die upon the Cross; a drop of blood, a single tear, would have been sufficient, but Jesus Christ willed not only to redeem us, but also to show us the fullness of his love.

— ST. MAXIMILIAN KOLBE

Blood of Christ, incarnate Word of God, save us!

January 6

My God, my God, why have you forsaken me? Why are you so far from helping me, from the words of my groaning? O my God, I cry by day, but you do not answer; and by night, but find no rest.

— PSALM 22:1–2

O good Jesus, hear me; within Your wounds, hide me.

January 7

We imitate Christ's death by being buried with him in baptism. If we ask what this kind of burial means and what benefit we may hope to derive from it, it means first of all making a complete break from our former way of life, and our Lord himself said this cannot be done unless a man is born again.

— St. Basil

You sit upon a great throne, Son of God, deliver us!

January 8

The Paschal mystery of Christ's Cross and Resurrection stands at the center of the Good News that the apostles, and the Church following them, are to proclaim to the world. God's saving plan was accomplished "once for all" by the redemptive death of his Son Jesus Christ.

— Catechism of the Catholic Church

Christ, Your death destroyed the one who had the power of death. Be our champion!

January 9

The Passion of our Lord and Savior Jesus Christ is the hope of glory and a lesson in patience. Brethren, let us then fearlessly acknowledge, and even openly proclaim, that Christ was crucified for us; let us confess it, not in fear but in joy, not in shame but in glory.

— St. Augustine of Hippo

Lord, suffer me not to be separated from You!

January 10

"**My soul is very sorrowful, even to death; remain here, and watch with me.**" And going a little farther he fell on his face and prayed. "**My father, if it is possible, let this chalice pass from me; nevertheless, not as I will, but as you will.**"

— Matthew 26:38–39

Lord, in the hour of my death, call me!

January 11

Now Christ suffered, not as in a delirium or in excitement, or in inadvertency, rather, he looked pain in the face! He offered his whole mind to it, and received it, as it were, directly into his bosom, and suffered all he suffered with a full consciousness of suffering.

— ST. JOHN HENRY NEWMAN

Precious Blood of Jesus, Divine Charity, set us free!

January 12

He allows himself to be bound, then led from tribunal to tribunal, and finally nailed to the Cross, and that without offering the least resistance, without making one complaint. Learn from so great a model the characters of perfect obedience to the will of God — that is, docility, promptitude and constancy.

— ST. IGNATIUS OF LOYOLA

Jesus, Son of the living God, have mercy on us!

January 13

These words of Jesus, "**Love one another, even as I have loved you**," should be not only a light to us, but they should also be a flame consuming the selfishness which prevents the growth of holiness. Jesus "loved us to the end," to the very limit of love: the Cross.

— St. Teresa of Calcutta

May the Sacred Heart of Jesus be loved in every place!

January 14

In his most sacred Passion, Jesus gave us an admirable example of a new form of silence: *silence in pain.*

— Servant of God Luis Martinez

From the fear of being despised, deliver me, Jesus!

January 15

I do the most for God's greater glory when I hold my tongue and suffer like Jesus, who died on the Cross, deprived of everything. Doing and suffering are the greatest proofs of love.

— St. Anthony Mary Claret

Heart of Jesus, salvation of those who trust in you, have mercy on us!

January 16

Jesus Christ suffers and dies to honor his Father by his extreme humiliation. There is no humiliation greater than that of the Cross. He suffers and dies to expiate sin. There is no expiation more appropriate than that of the Cross. He suffers and dies in order to heal and save sinners. There is no more efficacious remedy than that of the Cross. Let us always keep before our eyes the truth, the holiness, and the efficacy of the sufferings of Christ.

— Blessed William Joseph Chaminade

Heart of Jesus, house of God and gate of Heaven, have mercy on us!

January 17

But we see Jesus, who for a little while was made lower than the angels, crowned with glory and honor because of the suffering of death, so that by the grace of God he might taste death for every one. For it was fitting that he, for whom and by whom all things exist, in bringing many sons to glory, should make the pioneer of their salvation perfect through suffering.

— HEBREWS 2:9–10

God the Father of Heaven, have mercy on us!

January 18

If you are a Simon of Cyrene, take up your cross and follow Christ. If you are crucified beside him like one of the thieves, now, like the good thief, acknowledge your God. For your sake, and because of your sin, Christ himself was regarded as a sinner; for his sake, therefore, you must cease to sin. Worship him who was hung on the Cross because of you, even if you are hanging there yourself.

— ST. GREGORY NAZIANZEN

Soul of Christ, sanctify me!

January 19

One ounce of the Cross is worth more than a million pounds of prayer. One day of crucifixion is worth more than a hundred years of all other exercises. It is worth more to remain a moment upon the Cross, than to taste the delights of Paradise.

— VENERABLE MARIA VITTORIA ANGELINI

By Thy infinite love, deliver us, O Lord!

January 20

Truly, it is not right for us to refrain from tears, because
on the back of the Incarnate Son of God, we have laid an
enormous pile of evil deeds. We have constructed out of our
crimes a gibbet for him, and we have stretched out our iniquities upon him. Although out of love for us, he himself most
bravely carried and fully expiated them, yet we still decline
to carry out of love for him [our] little crosses, insignificant
afflictions. Either we avoid them, or we rush through them
with many complaints and sometimes shameful impatience.
Did we expect that we would enter into a different glory while
partying, drinking, indulging ourselves, when even the King
himself obtained glory through his suffering?

— ST. STANISLAUS PAPCZYŃSKI

Jesus, our God, have mercy on us!

January 21

He healed our physical infirmities by miracles; he freed us from our sins, many and grievous as they were, by suffering and dying, taking them upon himself as if he were answerable for them, sinless though he was.

— St. Maximus the Confessor

Blood of Christ, strength of confessors, save us!

January 22

Today Jesus said to me, **I desire that you know more profoundly the love that burns in My Heart for souls, and you will understand this when you meditate upon My Passion. Call upon My mercy on behalf of sinners; I desire their salvation. When you say this prayer, with a contrite heart and with faith on behalf of some sinner, I will give him the grace of conversion. This is the prayer: "O Blood and Water, which gushed forth from the Heart of Jesus as a fount of Mercy for us, I trust in You."**

— Jesus to St. Faustina Kowalska

Jesus, our refuge, have mercy on us!

January 23

In the Cross lies our salvation, our life; in the Cross we have a defense against our foes. In the Cross we have a pouring-in of heavenly sweetness, a strengthening of our minds and spiritual joy. In the Cross is the peak of virtue, the perfection of holiness. There is no salvation for our souls, no hope of life everlasting, but in the Cross.

— THOMAS À KEMPIS

Heart of my Jesus, depth of all virtue, have mercy on us!

January 24

Be sure, my child, that the heart of our most dear Lord beheld you from the tree of the Cross and loved you, and by that love he won for you all good things that you were ever to have, and amongst them your good resolutions.

— ST. FRANCIS DE SALES

Heart of Jesus, glowing with love for us, have mercy on us!

January 25

For the word of the Cross is folly to those who are perishing, but to us who are being saved it is the power of God. For Jews demand signs and Greeks seek wisdom, but we preach Christ crucified, a stumbling block to Jews and folly to Gentiles, but to those who are called, both Jews and Greeks, Christ the power of God and the wisdom of God. For the foolishness of God is wiser than men, and the weakness of God is stronger than men.

— 1 CORINTHIANS 1:18, 22–25

Jesus, eternal wisdom, have mercy on us!

January 26

If we desire to die a good death, we must lead a Christian life. And the way for us to prepare for a good death is to model our deaths upon the death of Jesus Christ. Can the life of a good Christian be anything other than that of a man nailed to the Cross with Jesus Christ?

— ST. JOHN VIANNEY

All Holy Priests, pray for us!

January 27

During the afternoon services at the Cathedral I preached on the Passion of Jesus. The Cathedral was full of people, just as it had been during all the sermons on the Passion. The people must like these sermons. It seems that this is what they want to hear, since they have had enough sermons on political and ethnic topics. Whoever wants politics can go to a political meeting. The people are happy to get a respite, in church at least, to hear the Word of God, to calm down and turn inward to meditate on their eternal salvation.

— BLESSED GEORGE MATULAITIS

By Your agony and Passion, deliver us, O Jesus!

January 28

No sin can be forgiven save by the power of Christ's Passion: hence the Apostle says (Heb. 9:22) that "without shedding of blood there is no remission." Consequently no movement of the human will suffices for the remission of sin, unless there be faith in Christ's Passion, and for the purpose of participating in it, either by receiving Baptism, or by submitting to the keys of the Church.

— ST. THOMAS AQUINAS

All you holy Doctors, pray for us!

January 29

I saw how unwillingly the Lord Jesus came to certain souls in Holy Communion. And he spoke these words to me: **I enter into certain hearts as into a second Passion.**

— JESUS TO ST. FAUSTINA KOWALSKA

Body of Christ, save us!

January 30

Then Pilate took Jesus and scourged him. And the soldiers plaited a crown of thorns, and put it on his head, and clothed him in a purple robe; they came up to him, saying, "Hail, King of the Jews!" and struck him with their hands.

— JOHN 19:1–3

Jesus, King of glory, have mercy on us!

January 31

[Many Christians in Church are] voluntarily distracted, showing neither modesty, attention, nor respect, standing [at times for kneeling] and gazing here and there. They do not assist at the Divine Sacrifice like Mary and St. John.

— ST. JOHN BOSCO

Blood of Christ, Victor over demons, save us!

FEBRUARY

February 1

Music of the Cross – how beautiful when mastered!
— BLESSED SOLANUS CASEY

Rest of the afflicted, save us, O holy Cross!

February 2

"Father, if you are willing, remove this chalice from me; nevertheless not my will, but yours, be done." And there appeared to him an angel from heaven, strengthening him. And being in agony he prayed more earnestly; and his sweat became like great drops of blood falling down upon the ground.
— LUKE 22:42–44

Blood of Christ, falling upon the earth in agony, save us!

February 3

The best book of meditations on the Passion is the Passion itself in the Gospel: read this and meditate upon it, reflecting upon the love and patience of Jesus Christ.

— ST. CLAUDE DE LA COLOMBIÈRE

All for Thee, Most Sacred Heart of Jesus!

February 4

The sign of the Cross is the most terrible weapon against the devil. Thus the Church wishes not only that we should have it continually in front of our minds to recall to us just what our souls are worth and what they cost Jesus Christ, but also that we should make it at every juncture ourselves: when we go to bed, when we awaken during the night, when we get up, when we begin any action, and, above all, when we are tempted.

— ST. JOHN VIANNEY

From all evil, deliver us, O Jesus!

February 5

A true virgin, she [St. Agatha] wore the glow of a pure conscience and the crimson of the Lamb's blood for her cosmetics. Again and again she meditated on the death of her eager lover. For her, Christ's death was recent, his blood was still moist. Her robe is the mark of her faithful witness to Christ. It bears the indelible marks of his crimson blood and the shining threads of her eloquence.

— St. Methodius of Sicily

Ocean of the Blood of Christ, set us free!

February 6

For the Eucharist represents the Passion by the perfect identity of the one who is offered in it and the one who was offered on the Cross, which is none other than the same Jesus Christ. The Sign of the Cross, however, represents the Passion by a simple motion that reproduces the form and shape of the Crucifixion.

— St. Francis de Sales

By Your most divine life, deliver us, O Jesus!

February 7

Jesus told me that I please him best by meditating on his sorrowful Passion, and by such meditation much light falls upon my soul. He who wants to learn true humility should reflect upon the Passion of Jesus. When I meditate upon the Passion of Jesus, I get a clear understanding of many things I could not comprehend before. I want to resemble you, O Jesus — you crucified, tortured, and humiliated. Jesus, imprint upon my heart and soul your own humility. I love you, Jesus, to the point of madness, you who were crushed with suffering as described by the prophet [cf. Isaiah 53:2–9], as if he could not see the human form in you because of your great suffering. It is in this condition, Jesus, that I love you to the point of madness. O eternal and infinite God, what has love done to you?

— St. Faustina Kowalska

By Your sufferings, deliver us, O Jesus!

February 8

Crosses teach us, give us further merit, crush us, but at the same time they exalt us spiritually and teach us not to trust our own skills and strength, but only the Immaculata. That is why God in his mercy sends these crosses.

— ST. MAXIMILIAN KOLBE

From the desire of being esteemed, deliver me, Jesus!

February 9

Two furious ruffians, who were thirsting for his blood, begin in the most barbarous manner to scourge his sacred body from head to foot. Our loving Lord, the Son of God, true God and true Man, writhed as a worm under the blows of these barbarians; his mild but deep groans might be heard from afar; they resounded through the air, forming a kind of touching accompaniment to the hissing of the instruments of torture. These groans resembled rather a touching cry of prayer and supplication than moans of anguish.

— BLESSED ANNE CATHERINE EMMERICH

Blood of Christ, shed profusely in the Scourging, save us!

February 10

Suffering will never be completely absent from our lives.
So don't be afraid of suffering. Your suffering is a great
means of love, if you make use of it, especially if you
offer it for peace in the world. Suffering in and of itself
is useless, but suffering that is shared with the Passion
of Christ is a wonderful gift and a sign of love. Christ's
suffering proved to be a gift, the greatest gift of love,
because through his sufferings our sins were atoned for.

— ST. TERESA OF CALCUTTA

Jesus, by the piercing of Thy Sacred Heart, have mercy on us!

February 11

I turned to Mary and asked her to obtain for me the grace
to imitate Our Lord's Heart. I saw how perfectly her heart
copied his: she loved those who put her Son to death and
offered him to God the Father for them. This enkindled a
very great love of virtue in my heart.

— ST. CLAUDE DE LA COLOMBIÈRE

Heart of Jesus, overflowing with goodness and love,
have mercy on us!

February 12

One day Blessed Angela Foligno begged Our Lord to let her know by which religious exercise she could honor him best. He appeared to her nailed to his Cross and said: **"My daughter, look at my wounds."** She then realized that nothing pleases our dear Lord more than meditation upon his sufferings.

— St. Louis de Montfort

Blood of Christ, of the new and eternal Covenant, save us!

February 13

But I am a worm, and no man; scorned by men, and despised by the people. All who see me mock me and wag their heads; "He committed his cause to the Lord, let him deliver him, let him rescue him, for he delights in him."

— Psalm 22:6–8

Jesus, You surround us with deliverance, have mercy on us!

February 14

I see every abasement of your soul, and nothing escapes My attention. I lift up the humble even to My very throne, because I want it so.

— JESUS TO ST. FAUSTINA KOWALSKA

Jesus, Lover of us, have mercy on us!

February 15

Our Lord could have worked the redemption of mankind with one word; he could have atoned for our sins by one prayer to the Father; he could have satisfied justice by the Incarnation alone, and by taking upon himself the sins of the human race. But such satisfaction would not have shown sufficiently either the immensity of evil contained in sin, or the infinite mercy of God.

— BLESSED MICHAEL SOPOĆKO

Sacred Heart of Jesus, I believe in Thy love for me!

February 16

Conceal yourselves in Jesus crucified, and hope for nothing
except that all men be thoroughly converted to his will.
— St. John of the Cross

Heart of Jesus, King and Center of all hearts, have mercy on us!

February 17

When his hour comes, he lives out the unique event of history
which does not pass away: Jesus dies, is buried, rises from the
dead, and is seated at the right hand of the Father "once for
all." His Paschal mystery is a real event that occurred in our
history, but it is unique: all other historical events happened
once, and then they passed away, swallowed up in the past.
The Paschal mystery of Christ, by contrast, cannot remain
only in the past, because by his death he destroyed death, and
all that Christ is — all that he did and suffered for men —
participates in the divine eternity, and so transcends all times
while being made present in them all. The event of the Cross
and Resurrection abides and draws everything toward life.
— Catechism of the Catholic Church

Holy Trinity, one God, have mercy on us!

February 18

The mark of mercy and friendship extended by the Victim should have moved Judas to repentance. The Divine Mediator, knowing all that would befall him, gave the order to Judas to open the curtain wider on the tragedy of Calvary. What Judas was to do, let him do quickly. The Lamb of God was ready for sacrifice.

— VENERABLE FULTON J. SHEEN

Jesus, True Light, have mercy on us!

February 19

I know from my own experience that the best way to avoid falling is to lean on the Cross of Jesus, with confidence in him alone who for our salvation desired to be nailed to it.

— ST. PADRE PIO

Jesus, Crown of Saints, have mercy on us!

February 20

Our poor dear Lord! I'll never sin again! I don't want
Our Lord to suffer any more!
— ST. JACINTA MARTO

Heart of Jesus, atonement for our sins, have mercy on us!

February 21

Cling to Jesus' holy Cross: let your soul be soaked in his
precious blood, then say: Oh, endless good, I accept this
suffering, as you want this.
— ST. PAUL OF THE CROSS

Blood of Christ, consolation of the dying, save us!

February 22

"Behold, the Lamb of God!"
— ST. JOHN THE BAPTIST

*Lamb of God, who takes away the sins of the world,
graciously hear us, O Lord!*

February 23

The life of men is a pilgrimage, continual, long and wearisome. Up and up along the steep and stony road, the road marked out for all upon that hill. In this mystery (The Way of the Cross) Jesus represents the whole race of men. Every one of us must have his own cross to bear; otherwise, tempted by selfishness or cruelty, we should sooner or later fall by the roadside. From the contemplation of Jesus climbing up to Calvary we learn, first with our hearts and then with our minds, to embrace and kiss the Cross, and bear it bravely and with joy.

— POPE ST. JOHN XXIII

From the desire of being honored, deliver me, Jesus!

February 24

"Now the salvation and the power and the kingdom
of our God and the authority of his Christ have come,
for the accuser of our brethren has been thrown down,
who accuses them day and night before our God. And
they have conquered him by the blood of the Lamb and
by the word of their testimony, for they loved not their
lives even onto death. Rejoice then, O heaven and you
that dwell therein!"

— REVELATION 12:10–12

Lamb of God, spare us, O Lord!

February 25

It was fitting that when the hour of the Passion was to
come, Christ should institute a new Sacrament after
celebrating the old.

— ST. THOMAS AQUINAS

Jesus, Author of Life, have mercy on us!

February 26

What our Blessed Lord contemplated in his agony was not just the buffeting of soldiers, and the pinioning of his hands and feet to a bar of contradiction, but rather the awful burden of the world's sin, and the fact that the world was about to spurn his Father by rejecting him.

— VENERABLE FULTON J. SHEEN

Precious Blood of Jesus Christ, Power of Christians, set us free!

February 27

Let us make a resolution to have a great respect for all the crosses, which are blessed, and which represent to us in a small way all that our God suffered for us. Let us recall that from the Cross flow all the graces that are bestowed upon us and that, as a consequence, a cross which is blessed is a source of blessings, that we should often make the Sign of the Cross on ourselves and always with great respect, and, finally, that our homes should never remain without this symbol of salvation.

— ST. JOHN VIANNEY

Lift high the Cross!

February 28

There is more merit to one hour of meditation on My sorrowful Passion than there is to a whole year of flagellation that draws blood; the contemplation of My painful wounds is of great profit to you, and it brings Me great joy.

— Jesus to St. Faustina Kowalska

Jesus, zealous lover of souls, have mercy on us!

February 29

His heart, burning with love for souls who forced him onto the Cross, remains with us in the Eucharist and desires to enter our hearts.

— St. Maximilian Kolbe

Eucharistic Jesus, save us!

MARCH

March 1

Jesus looked at me and said, **Souls perish in spite of My
bitter Passion. I am giving them the last hope of salvation;
that is, the Feast of My Mercy. If they will not adore My
mercy, they will perish for all eternity. Secretary of My
mercy, write, tell souls about this great mercy of Mine,
because the awful day, the day of My justice, is near.**

— JESUS TO ST. FAUSTINA KOWALSKA

Heart of Jesus, patient and full of mercy, have mercy on us!

March 2

Pilate was one of those who believed that truth was not objective but subjective, that each man determined for himself what was to be true. It is often the fault of practical men, such as Pilate, to regard the search for objective truth as useless theorizing. Skepticism is not an intellectual position; it is a moral position, in the sense that it is determined not so much by reason as by the way one acts and behaves. Pilate's desire to save Jesus was due to a kind of liberalism which combined disbelief in Absolute Truth with a half-benevolent unwillingness to disturb such dreamers and their superstitions. Pilate asked the question, "What is truth?" of the only person in the world who could answer it in all its fullness.

— VENERABLE FULTON J. SHEEN

Sweet Heart of Jesus, be my love!

March 3

Is it nothing to you, all you who pass by? Look and see if there is any sorrow like my sorrow which was brought upon me, which the Lord inflicted on the day of his fierce anger.

— LAMENTATIONS 1:12

Thine aid supply, Thy strength bestow!

March 4

You see, the Cross is at the root of everything; everything is based upon our dying there. There is no other road to life, to true inward peace, but the road of the Cross, of dying daily to self. Walk where you will, seek whatever you have in mind to; you will find no higher road above, no safer road below, than the road of the holy Cross.

— THOMAS À KEMPIS

Blood of Christ, relief of the burdened, save us!

March 5

Think of the comfort that Veronica's action means to Jesus. It is not much; his face is covered again with blood, sweat, and the dust of the road. What really matters to him is her care, her love, and her desire to help. She does not mind what might happen to her, what people might say about her for helping Jesus. Her reward is great!

— SERVANT OF GOD IDA PETERFY

God's power, guide me!

March 6

Her [Mary's] sacrificial participation, which began with the Incarnation of the Word of God, will not cease until Calvary. She is the inseparable companion and collaborator of her Son throughout her earthly life. She doesn't let herself be frightened by the most critical moments; she follows her beloved Son in the work of redemption. She ascends with him to Calvary and there she offers him and herself to God. She stands at the foot of the cross united with him in his death, and not for a moment does she retreat from her sacrifice.

— BLESSED GEORGE KASZYRA

Son of God, You are the King of Kings and Lord of Lords. Deliver us!

March 7

There is no better test to distinguish the chaff from the grain, in the Church of God, than the manner in which sufferings, contradictions, and contempt are borne. Whoever remains unmoved under these, is grain. Whoever rises against them is chaff; and the lighter and more worthless he is, the higher he rises — that is, the more he is agitated, and the more proudly he replies.

— ST. AUGUSTINE OF HIPPO

Precious Blood of Jesus Christ, Power of the Holy Spirit, save us!

March 8

As they were gathered in Galilee, Jesus said to them, **"The Son of Man is to be delivered into the hands of men, and they will kill him, and he will be raised on the third day."** And they were greatly distressed.

— MATTHEW 17:22–23

Worthy is the Lamb who was slain, to receive power, glory, and honor!

March 9

The love of God — God's power — is stronger than the powers of destruction. This very "going out," this setting on the path of the Passion, when Jesus steps outside the boundary of the protective walls of the city, is a gesture of victory. The mystery of Gethsemane already holds within it the mystery of Easter joy. Jesus is the "stronger man." There is no power that can withstand him now; no place where he is not to be found. He summons us to dare to accompany him on his path; for where faith and love are, he is there, and the power of peace is there which overcomes nothingness and death.

— POPE BENEDICT XVI

No demonic power can separate us from Your love.
Jesus, Your heart is our refuge!

March 10

If it were not for the priest, the Passion and Death of Jesus would not be of any help to us. What good would a chest full of gold be if there were no one to open it? The priest has the key to the heavenly treasures.

— ST. JOHN VIANNEY

By Your glory, deliver us, O Jesus!

March 11

Today, I feel a great capacity for suffering: I am conscious to some extent of the strength and serenity of my dear Master at the time of his Passion. Souls! Souls! Souls! I want them all to belong to God. I do not want a single one to escape the Savior. I want each one to respond to the Creator's designs for her. I want to plunge impious, blind hatred into pure, atoning love. I want to annihilate evil in the Blood of the infinite Lamb.

— BLESSED DINA BÉLANGER

Jesus, most amiable, have mercy on us!

March 12

Then Jesus, crying with a loud voice, said, **"Father, into your hands I commit my spirit!"** And having said this, he breathed his last. Now when the centurion saw what had taken place, he praised God, and said, "Certainly this man was innocent!" And all the multitudes who assembled to see the sight, when they saw what had taken place, returned home beating their breasts.

— LUKE 23:46–48

Jesus, mighty God, have mercy on us!

March 13

The prince of this world rejoices when someone renounces the Cross, for well does he know that the confession of the Cross is his defeat, inasmuch as it is the sign of the victory over his power: he is frightened to see it and fears to hear it.

— ST. IGNATIUS OF ANTIOCH

Salvation of the world, save us, O holy Cross!

March 14

When I become immersed in the Lord's Passion, I often see
the Lord Jesus, during adoration, in this manner: after the
scourging, the torturers took the Lord and stripped Him of
his own garment, which had already adhered to the wounds;
as they took it off, His wounds reopened; then they threw a
dirty and tattered scarlet cloak over the fresh wounds of the
Lord. The cloak, in some places, barely reached His knees.
They made Him sit on a piece of beam. And then they wove
a crown of thorns, which they put on his sacred head. They
put a reed in His hand and made fun of Him, bowing to Him
as to a king. Some spat in His face, while others took the
reed and struck Him on the head with it. Others caused Him
pain by slapping him; still others covered His face and struck
Him with their fists. Jesus bore all this with meekness. Who
can comprehend Him — comprehend His suffering? Jesus'
eyes were downcast. I sensed what was happening in the most
sweet Heart of Jesus at that time. Let every soul reflect on
what Jesus was suffering at that moment. They tried to outdo
each other in insulting the Lord. I reflected: Where does such
malice in man come from? It is caused by sin.

— St. Faustina Kowalska

Heart of Jesus, ridiculed and scorned, have mercy on us!

March 15

Such a promise was never made before, that a dead man would keep an appointment with his friends after three days in the tomb. Though the sheep would forsake the Shepherd, the Shepherd would find his sheep. As Adam lost the heritage of union with God in a garden, so now Our Blessed Lord ushered in its restoration in a garden. Eden and Gethsemane were the two gardens around which revolved the fate of humanity.

— VENERABLE FULTON J. SHEEN

By Your Agony and Crucifixion, Jesus, save Your people!

March 16

People who suffer in God's name help Jesus to carry the Cross and so they'll take part in his glory.

— ST. PAUL OF THE CROSS

God the Son, Redeemer of the world, have mercy on us!

March 17

I bind myself today to the virtue of the incarnation of Christ
with his baptism, the virtue of his crucifixion with his burial,
the virtue of his resurrection with his ascension, the virtue of
his coming on the Judgment Day.

— St. Patrick

From the fear of being wronged, deliver me, Jesus!

March 18

The birds have nests and the foxes have lairs, but Jesus doesn't
even have a stone on which to lay his head. For his birth, he
had a manger; for his death, he had a cross.

— St. Anthony Mary Claret

Jesus, most obedient, have mercy on us!

March 19

The birth of Jesus, the death of Joseph, moments of unutterable sweetness, unparalleled in the history of mankind. Saint Joseph went to the bosom of Abraham, to wait his time, out of God's presence. Jesus had to preach, suffer, and die; Mary to witness his sufferings, and, even after he had risen again, to go on living without him amid the changes of life and the heartlessness of the heathen. The birth of Jesus, the death of Joseph, those moments of tranquility pure, and perfect and living sympathy, between the three members of this earthly Trinity, were its beginning and its end.

— St. John Henry Newman

St. Joseph, most courageous, pray for us!

March 20

How precious must the resolutions be that are the fruits of our Lord's Passion! And how dear to my heart, since they were dear to that of Jesus! Savior of my soul, You died to win them for me; grant me the grace sooner to die than forget them.

— St. Francis de Sales

Jesus, most admirable, have mercy on us!

March 21

But in the midst of this excitement the invincible Queen,
though filled with the bitterest sorrow, preserved her
constancy and composure, praying for the unbelievers
and the evil—doers, as if she had no other care than to
implore grace and pardon for their sins. She loved them
as sincerely as if she were receiving favors and blessings
at their hands. She permitted no indignation or anger to
arise in her heart against the sacrilegious ministers of the
Passion and Death of her beloved Son, not any sign of
such feelings in her exterior conduct.

— Venerable Mary of Ágreda

Mary, Mother of Jesus of Nazareth, pray for us!

March 22

Let us run to accompany him as he hastens toward his
Passion, and imitate those who met him then, not by
covering his path with garments, olive branches or palms,
but by doing all we can to prostrate ourselves before him
by being humble and trying to live as he would wish.
Then we shall be able to receive the Word at his coming,
and God, whom no limits can contain, will be within us.

— St. Andrew of Crete

Sanctify Your people, redeemed by Your Blood!

March 23

Suffering, pain, sorrow, humiliation, feelings of loneliness, are
nothing but the kiss of Jesus, a sign that you have come so
close that he can kiss you. Remember that the Passion of Christ
ends always in the joy of the resurrection of Christ, so when
you feel in your own heart the suffering of Christ, remember
the resurrection has to come. Never let anything so fill you
with sorrow as to make you forget the joy of Christ risen.

— St. Teresa of Calcutta

Heart of Jesus, source of life and holiness, have mercy on us!

March 24

What is more sweet to a soul that loves God, than to suffer for him? She knows that, by cheerfully embracing sufferings she pleases God, and that her pains shall be the brightest jewels in her crown in paradise. And who is there that will not suffer and die in imitation of Jesus Christ, who has gone before us carrying his Cross, to offer himself in sacrifice for the love of us, and inviting us to follow his example?

— St. Alphonsus Liguori

Jesus, treasure of the faithful, have mercy on us!

March 25

Then I saw him bearing the Cross, which he embraced and kissed with infinite love, like a companion longed for and desired, like the trophy of his victory. Its weight was enormous; I extended my arms to take it, and in my heart I longed to console him, and as much as I could, to encounter him at the turn of a corner, to approach him looking at me, to kiss his face a thousand times with my spirit, his face which was imprinted on my soul long before it was imprinted on Veronica's veil — oh, yes, indelibly engraved! His adorable face!

— MARY TO BLESSED CONCEPCIÓN CABRERA DE ARMIDA

Heart of Jesus, formed by the Holy Spirit in the womb of the Virgin Mother, have mercy on us!

March 26

Beneath the Cross one learns to love.
— ST. PADRE PIO

Jesus, Lover of chastity, have mercy on us!

March 27

Every day, and often, especially in difficult moments, look upon the Crucified and learn, most impoverished one, to follow the Lord Jesus in all suffering, however great, and in all the contempt to which you are subject. Be obedient to God in all things. Love your enemies the more, in fact love them all the more when they cause you pain, for Jesus said: "Father forgive them, for they know not what they do."

— ST. MAXIMILIAN KOLBE

From the desire of being esteemed, deliver me, Jesus!

March 28

Judas came, one of the Twelve, and with him a crowd with swords and clubs, from the chief priests and the scribes and the elders. Now the betrayer had given them a sign, saying, "The one I shall kiss is the man; seize him and lead him away safely." And when he came, he went up to him at once, and said, "Master!" And he kissed him. And they laid hands on him and seized him.

— MARK 14:43–46

Your sharp sword strikes the nations, Son of God. Deliver us!

March 29

What is the Cross? The crushing weight of all the sins of the world. Jesus' sorrow surpasses all bounds. But by virtue of the love of the Divine Heart, the Cross is changed into a torrent of all good, into an inexhaustible fountain of happiness.

— SERVANT OF GOD LUIS MARTINEZ

Sweet Heart of my Jesus, grant that I may ever love Thee more!

March 30

Christ would not drink the drugged cup which was offered to Him to cloud His mind. He willed to have the full sense of pain. His soul was so intently fixed on His suffering as not to be distracted from it; and it was so active, and recollected the past and anticipated the future, and the whole passion was, as it were, concentrated on each moment of it, and all that He had suffered and all that He was to suffer lent its aid to increase what He was suffering.

— ST. JOHN HENRY NEWMAN

Jesus, by Thy Sacred Wounds, deliver us!

March 31

The witness of the Cross and resurrection of Christ have handed onto the Church and to mankind a specific Gospel of suffering. The Redeemer himself wrote this Gospel, above all by his own suffering accepted in love, so that man "should not perish but have eternal life [John 3:16]." This suffering, together with the living word of his teaching, became a rich source for all those who shared in Jesus' sufferings among the first generation of his disciples and confessors, and among those who have come after them down the centuries.

— POPE ST. JOHN PAUL II

He came that we might have life! Rejoice!

APRIL

April 1

It is he who endured every kind of suffering in all those
who foreshadowed him. In Abel, he was slain, in Isaac
bound, in Jacob exiled, in Joseph sold, in Moses exposed
to die. He was sacrificed in the Passover lamb, persecuted
in David, dishonored in the prophets.

— St. Melito of Sardis

From the fear of being ridiculed, deliver me, Jesus!

April 2

Death is certain; life is short and vanishes like the smoke. Fix
your minds, then, on the Passion of our Lord Jesus Christ.
Inflamed with love for us, he came down from heaven to
redeem us. For our sake he endured every torment of body
and soul and shrank from no bodily pain. He himself gave us
an example of perfect patience and love.

— St. Francis of Paola

Save us, O holy Cross!

April 3

Let us fix our attention on the blood of Christ and recognize how precious it is to God his Father, since it was shed for our salvation and brought the grace of repentance to all the world.

— POPE ST. CLEMENT I

God the Father of Heaven,
cover us with the Precious Blood of Thy Son!

April 4

Those animal sacrifices foreshadowed the flesh of Christ which he would offer for our sins, though himself without sin, and the blood which he would pour out for the forgiveness of our sins. In this sacrifice there is thanksgiving for, and commemoration of, the flesh of Christ that he offered for us, and the blood that the same God poured out for us.

— ST. FULGENTIUS OF RUSPE

Your stripes have healed us. Jesus, Your Heart is our refuge!

April 5

The Lord sends us tribulation and infirmities to give us the means of paying the immense debts we have contracted with him. Therefore, those who have good sense receive them joyfully, for they think more of the good which they may derive from them than of the pain which they experience on account of them.

— St. Vincent Ferrer

By Thy ignominious death, O Lord, deliver us!

April 6

We must now pass through the first veil and approach the second, turning our eyes toward the Holy of Holies. I will say more: we must sacrifice ourselves to God, each day and in everything we do, accepting his Passion by our sufferings, and honoring his blood by shedding our own. We must be ready to be crucified.

— St. Gregory Nazianzen

You have redeemed us, O Lord, in Your Blood, and made us, for our God, a kingdom!

April 7

Be driven by the love of God then, because Jesus Christ died for all, that those who live may live not for themselves but for him who died and rose for them. Let your students be moved by your untiring care for them and feel as though God were encouraging them through you, because you perform your duties as ambassadors of Christ.

— St. John Baptist de La Salle

Jesus, Teacher of the Evangelists, have mercy on us!

April 8

During one of the adorations, Jesus promised me that:
**With souls that have recourse to My mercy and with those
that glorify and proclaim My great mercy to others, I
will deal according to My infinite mercy at the hour of
their death. My Heart is sorrowful,** Jesus said, **because
even chosen souls do not understand the greatness of My
mercy. Their relationship [with Me] is, in certain ways,
imbued with mistrust. Oh, how much that wounds My
Heart! Remember My Passion, and if you do not believe
My words, at least believe My wounds.**

— JESUS TO ST. FAUSTINA KOWALSKA

Heart of Jesus, obedient to death, have mercy on us!

April 9

The high priest then questioned Jesus about his disciples and his teaching. Jesus answered him, **"I have spoken openly to the world; I have always taught in the synagogues and in the temple, where all Jews come together; I have said nothing secretly. Why do you ask me? Ask those who have heard me, what I said to them; they know what I said."** When he had said this, one of the officers standing by struck Jesus with his hand, saying, "Is that how you answer the high priest?" Jesus answered him, **"If I have spoken wrongly, bear witness to the wrong, but if I have spoken rightly, why do you strike me?"**

— JOHN 18:19–23

By Thy bonds and chains, O Lord, deliver us!

April 10

When Pontius Pilate governed the province of Judea, under Tiberius Caesar, Christ the Lord was nailed to a cross. Having been seized, mocked, outraged and tortured in various forms, he was finally crucified. It cannot be a matter of doubt that his soul, as to its inferior part, was sensible of these torments; for as he really assumed human nature, it is a necessary consequence that he really, and in his soul, experienced a most acute sense of pain.

— THE CATECHISM OF THE COUNCIL OF TRENT

Jesus, meek and humble of Heart, have mercy on us!

April 11

There is only one recorded time in the history of our Blessed Lord when he sang, and that was after the Last Supper when he went out to his death in the Garden of Gethsemane.

— VENERABLE FULTON J. SHEEN

Precious Blood of Jesus Christ, Boldness of the Children of God, save us!

April 12

And what are the causes of this desolation of the Savior?
The eternal misery that sin is preparing for us; this is cause
of his fear. The infinite injury that sin does to the majesty
of his Father; this is the cause of his sorrow. The useless-
ness of his sufferings for so many miserable creatures
who persist in the way of perdition; this is the cause of
his weariness. The sight of God basely insulted, and of so
many souls miserably damned, is the cause of his agony.
Return to yourself. You see what Jesus Christ suffered on
your account and for you: what will you do for him?

— ST. IGNATIUS OF LOYOLA

Blood of Jesus Christ, pledge of eternal life, save us!

April 13

The way is narrow. Whoever expects to walk in it with
ease must be detached from all things, leaning on the staff
of the Cross; that is, firmly resolving to be willing to suffer
all things for love of God.

— ST. JOHN OF THE CROSS

Thou who savest by Thy grace, we beseech Thee, hear us!

April 14

They covered his face and thus shut out the light of heaven; and yet in covering his eyes, it was their own they blinded. The veil was really on their hearts, not on his eyes. They who were so proud of their earthly temple now buffeted the Heavenly Temple, for in him dwelt the fullness of the Godhead. They used the title "Christ" sarcastically; but they were more right than they knew, for he was the Messiah, the Anointed of God.

— Venerable Fulton J. Sheen

Heart of Jesus, most worthy of all praise, have mercy on us!

April 15

It is not enough that you [Jesus] do this, but to point out to me more closely how deeply you love me, you came down from heaven of purest joys into this sullied valley of tears; you spent your life in poverty and amid sufferings and deprivation and, finally, abused and rejected, an object of ridicule, you will to hang upon the ignominious gibbet of the Cross in the company of two thieves. In this terrifying and sacrificial manner, you, O God of Love, redeemed me!

— St. Maximilian Kolbe

From the desire of being praised, deliver me, Jesus!

April 16

Remember that the priest at the altar is always Jesus Christ on the Cross.

— St. Bernadette Soubirous

Jesus Christ Crucified, have mercy on us!

April 17

It's in the Passion of Jesus Christ that the soul gets the milk and the sweet honey of holy love.

— St. Paul of the Cross

At your name every knee shall bow in heaven and on earth and under the earth. Jesus, we love you!

April 18

Behold, my servant shall prosper, he shall be exalted and lifted up, and shall be very high. As many were astonished at him — his appearance was so marred, beyond human semblance, and his form beyond that of the sons of men – so shall he startle many nations; kings shall shut their mouths because of him; for that which has not been told them they shall see, and that which they have not heard they shall understand.

— ISAIAH 52:13–15

O saving Victim, opening wide the
gates of heaven to man below!

April 19

The Cross on Calvary, the Cross on which Christ conducts his final dialogue with the Father, emerges from the very heart of the love that man, created in the image and likeness of God, has been given as gift, according to God's eternal plan.

— POPE ST. JOHN PAUL II

Blood of Christ, peace and tenderness of hearts, save us!

April 20

Our Lord's sufferings were so great, because his soul was in suffering. What shows this is that his soul began to suffer before his bodily Passion, as we see in the agony of the garden. The first anguish which came upon his body was not from without — it was not from the scourges, the thorns, or the nails, but from his soul.

— ST. JOHN HENRY NEWMAN

From the fear of being ridiculed, deliver me, Jesus!

April 21

Humility, obedience, meekness, and love are the virtues that shine through the Cross and the Blessed Sacrament of the Altar. O my Jesus, help me imitate you!

— ST. ANTHONY MARY CLARET

By Your most divine life, deliver us, O Jesus!

April 22

Suffering in itself has no value. The greatest gift we can enjoy is the possibility to share Christ's Passion.

— St. Teresa of Calcutta

From every division in our family, we implore Thee, deliver us, O Lord!

April 23

Do you rejoice when he, with unheard of cruelty, is lashed on his whole body, is torn apart, and is pulled to pieces with the most dreadful whips, as if he was the most vicious evildoer? Alas, is it permissible for you to whip the Son of God? No one said these words when our most merciful Savior suffered at the pillar. Scarcely anyone could be found who was moved by pity for him, and no one would weep over him. Indeed, as many as were present, absorbed by this horrible spectacle, displayed such a cheerful countenance, as if wanting to testify that by his wounds they were particularly invigorated.

— St. Stanislaus Papczyński

Blood of Christ, stream of mercy, save us!

April 24

Whoever is truly patient wishes for all that God wishes, and
in the manner and with the inconveniences that he wishes; as
to works, one day of suffering borne with resignation is worth
more than a month of great labors; and as to prayer, which
is better: to remain upon the Cross with Christ, or to stay at
the foot of it and contemplate His sufferings? Besides, to offer
to the Lord his own weakness, to remember for whom it was
suffered, and to conform ourselves to his holy will, is certainly
a very excellent prayer.

— ST. FRANCIS DE SALES

Lord, grant us Your holy patience in our suffering!

April 25

And Pilate again said to them, "Then what shall I do with the man whom you call the King of the Jews?" And they cried out again, "Crucify him." And Pilate said to them, "Why, what evil has he done?" But they shouted all the more, "Crucify him." So Pilate, wishing to satisfy the crowd, released for them Barabbas; and after having scourged Jesus, he delivered him to be crucified.

— MARK 15:12–15

Saint Mark the Evangelist, pray for us!

April 26

God loves us in His Son; the painful Passion of the Son of God constantly turns aside the wrath of God.

— ST. FAUSTINA KOWALSKA

From Your wrath, deliver us, O Jesus.

April 27

No sooner did Caiaphas, with the other members of the Council, leave the tribunal than a crowd of miscreants — the very scum of the people — surround Jesus like a swarm of wasps, and began to heap every imaginable insult upon him. Even during the trial, while the witnesses were speaking, the archers and some others could not restrain their cruel inclinations, but pulled out handfuls of his hair and beard, spat upon him, struck him with their fists, wounded him with sharp-pointed sticks, and even ran needles into his body.

— BLESSED ANNE CATHERINE EMMERICH

Christ conquers! Christ reigns! Christ rules!

April 28

The Holy Sacrifice of the Mass gives boundless honor to the Most Blessed Trinity because it represents the Passion of Jesus Christ and because through the Mass we offer God the merits of our Lord's obedience, of his sufferings and of his Precious Blood. The whole of the heavenly court also receives joy from the Mass.

— St. Louis de Montfort

Blood of Christ, Eucharistic drink and refreshment of souls, save us!

April 29

My creatures should see and know that I wish nothing but their good, through the Blood of my only-begotten Son, in which they are washed from their iniquities. By this Blood they are enabled to know my Truth; how, in order to give them eternal life, I created them in my image and likeness and re-created them to grace with the Blood of my Son, making them sons of adoption.

— GOD THE FATHER TO ST. CATHERINE OF SIENA

Blood of Christ, flowing forth in the Crowning with Thorns, save us!

April 30

Consider Jesus' fiat in the garden ["**Not my will, but yours be done**" (Luke 22:42)]. What a weight he must have felt to have sweat, and to have sweat blood! Proclaim your fiat too, as much in propitious times as in adverse circumstances. Do not worry or wrestle with how you will be able to express it. We know that human nature avoids difficult things, like the cross, but that does not mean the soul is not submitted to God's will once it is understood.

— ST. PADRE PIO

God's might, uphold me!

MAY

May 1

How great a share had not the glorious St. Joseph in the chalice of Jesus' Passion, by the services which he rendered to his sacred humanity!

— St. Mary Magdalene de Pazzi

Saint Joseph, Terror of Demons, pray for us!

May 2

"My kingship is not of this world; if my kingdom were of this world, my servants would fight, that I might not be handed over to the Jews; but my kingship is not from this world." Pilate said to him, "So you are a king? Jesus answered, **"You say that I am a king. For this I was born, and for this I have come into the world, to bear witness to the truth. Every one who is of the truth hears my voice."** Pilate said to him, "What is truth?"

— John 18:36–38

By Thy crown of thorns, O Lord, save us!

May 3

Be ready, like the holy Redeemer was, to drink with him the dark water of the Kidron River, accepting tribulations and penance with devout resignation. Cross over the Kidron with Jesus, suffering the disdain of the world with constancy and courage out of love for Jesus. Always keep yourself recollected, and let your life be hidden in Jesus and with him in the Garden of Gethsemane, that is, in the silence of meditation and solitude, so that the flood of humiliations do not block your journey.

— ST. PADRE PIO

By Your sorrowful Passion, deliver us, O Jesus!

May 4

And they compelled a passer-by, Simon of Cyrene, who was coming in from the country, the father of Rufus, to carry his cross. And they brought him to the place called Golgotha (which means the place of the skull). And they offered him wine mingled with myrrh; but he did not take it. And they crucified him, and divided his garments among them, casting lots for them, to decide what each should take.

— MARK 15:21–25

Jesus, most amiable, have mercy on us!

May 5

To go to Mass means to go to Calvary to meet him, our Redeemer.

— POPE ST. JOHN PAUL II

From the fear of being forgotten, deliver me, Jesus!

May 6

Jesus Christ knew beforehand the trials that awaited him in the Garden of Olives; but it does not make him less faithful to the holy custom of retiring into solitude to pray. With what intrepidity and what peace he goes to the first theater of his bloody Passion! From this example of the Savior, learn fidelity to good resolutions in spite of obstacles and trials.

— ST. IGNATIUS OF LOYOLA

Christ, You crushed the serpent beneath Your heel.
We praise You!

May 7

Tradition narrates that Jesus, weighed down by his heavy Cross, had no sooner set out on the sorrowful Way of the Cross when Mary joined him from a street which opened onto it. In her dreadful agony of soul, the mother lifted her eyes to him, and his eyes met hers. Whoever is fortunate enough to make the Way of the Cross in Jerusalem will find the site of this encounter at the fourth station. A church has been built there dedicated to St. Mary of the Agony.

— BLESSED JAMES ALBERIONE

Jesus, by Thy shameful death on the Cross, have mercy on us!

May 8

He was despised and rejected by men; a man of sorrows, and acquainted with grief; and as one from whom men hide their faces he was despised, and we esteemed him not. Surely he has borne our griefs and carried our sorrows; yet we esteemed him stricken, struck down by God, and afflicted. But he was wounded for our transgressions, he was bruised for our iniquities; upon him was the chastisement that made us whole, and with his stripes we are healed.

— Isaiah 53:3–5

Blood of Christ, price of our salvation, save us!

May 9

I would like to help all souls, and especially consecrated souls, to understand the price of the Cross. Moral or physical suffering is an eternal goldmine; it is a flaming dart shot by love from the Heart of the Infinite to inflame the human heart and plunge it into the Divinity. The Cross! It is the dazzling scepter of incarnate Wisdom, the co-redeeming jewel of the immaculate Virgin, the radiant palm of the blessed.

— Blessed Dina Bélanger

Most Sacred Heart of Jesus, I believe in Your love for me!

May 10

It is necessary, therefore, that having represented to yourself the greatness of the pains [of hell] and their eternity, and having excited within yourself the fear of them and made a resolution to serve God better, you must then represent to yourself the Savior on the Cross and run to him with arms outstretched. Then embrace his feet with interior acclamations full of hope: "O door of my hopes, your blood will be my safeguard!" "I am yours, Lord, and you will save me!" Come to rest in this affliction, thanking our Savior for his blood, offering him to his Father for your deliverance and praying that the Father will grant it.

— St. Francis de Sales

In the day of judgment, we beseech Thee, hear us!

May 11

When Jesus was brought before the judgment seat of Pontius Pilate, he did not vanish. It was the crisis and the goal; it was the hour and the power of darkness. It was the supremely supernatural act, of all his miraculous life, that he did not vanish.

— G.K. Chesterton

Most Sacred Heart of Jesus, may Your holy will be done!

May 12

Although human nature was united to the Divine Person, he felt the bitterness of his Passion as acutely as if no such union had existed, because in the one Person of Jesus Christ were preserved the properties of both natures, human and divine; and therefore what was passible and mortal remained passible and mortal; while what was impassible and immortal, that is, his Divine Nature, continued impassible and immortal.

— THE CATECHISM OF THE COUNCIL OF TRENT

Jesus, true God and true Man, have mercy on us!

May 13

When Jesus saw his mother, and the disciple whom he loved standing near, he said to his mother, **"Woman, behold your son!"** Then he said to the disciple, **"Behold, your mother!"** And from that hour the disciple took her into his own home.

— JOHN 19:26–27

Jesus, Son of Mary, have mercy on us!

May 14

Besides these sufferings, our Lord during his time of teaching suffered even more morally, for he had to face open persecution from the Pharisees and priests, to endure every kind of insult and calumny from them. They called him a wine-bibber, a sinner, subversive, a seducer of the people, possessed by Beelzebub, an imposter and a sly Samaritan. Could anything have been more defamatory or more humiliating?

— BLESSED MICHAEL SOPOĆKO

The Heart of Jesus is with me! Thy Kingdom come!

May 15

The Cross is the most profound condescension of God to man and to what man — especially in difficult and painful moments — looks on as his unhappy destiny. The Cross is like a touch of eternal love upon the most painful wounds of man's earthly existence; it is the total fulfillment of the messianic program that Christ once formulated in the synagogue at Nazareth and then repeated to the messengers sent by John the Baptist.

— POPE ST. JOHN PAUL II

*Heart of Jesus, in whom the Father is well pleased,
have mercy on us!*

May 16

Although I was ill, I made up my mind to make a Holy Hour today as usual. During that hour, I saw the Lord Jesus being scourged at the pillar. In the midst of this frightful torture, Jesus was praying. After a while, He said to me, **There are few souls who contemplate My Passion with true feeling; I give great graces to souls who meditate devoutly on My Passion.**

— ST. FAUSTINA KOWALSKA

Jesus, most patient, have mercy on us!

May 17

Simon was much annoyed, and expressed the greatest vexation at being obliged to walk with a man in so deplorable a condition of dirt and misery; but Jesus wept, and cast such a mild and heavenly look upon him that he was touched. Simon had not carried the Cross after Jesus any length of time before he felt his heart deeply touched by grace.

— BLESSED ANNE CATHERINE EMMERICH

For the sake of His sorrowful Passion, have mercy on us and on the whole world!

May 18

In truth, I have such a great compassion for you, O so good and so sweet Jesus, for this battle taken up against our sins was so intense for you that this shower of your Blood was so abundantly drawn out from your Divine Body. But even so, I rejoice within my heart, and I am glad with the whole human race, that in the solitude of Gethsemane, your Blood sprang forth to become a bath, in which we may be washed from our filth.

— ST. STANISLAUS PAPCZYŃSKI

Blood of Christ, consolation of the dying, save us!

May 19

The fact that he suffered death precisely on the wood of the cross must also be attributed to a particular counsel of God, which decreed that life should return by the way whence death had arisen. The serpent who had triumphed over our first parents by the wood (of a tree) was vanquished by Christ on the wood of the Cross.

— THE CATECHISM OF THE COUNCIL OF TRENT

Christ, You love us and You save us!

May 20

Stripped of his garments one last time, he is hurriedly placed on the cross to which they fasten his hands and feet with large nails that make large wounds. Who could ever comprehend the horrible suffering at that moment? The suffering that comes from having feet and hands pierced all the way through by iron nails; from being fastened and hung in that way on a gibbet that, when raised up, is let fall into a hole hallowed out to hold its base; from hanging there three whole hours, at the end of which he was given the thrust of a lance that created in his side a large, deep wound, as if it were not enough for him to die from such an appalling torture. No, our minds cannot comprehend, and no voice could express such cruel pain.

— Blessed Basil Moreau

Son of God, deliver us!

May 21

Since all have sinned and fall short of the glory of God, they are justified by his grace as a gift, through the redemption which is in Christ Jesus, whom God put forward as an expiation by his blood, to be received by faith.

— ROMANS 3:23–25

Blood of Christ, poured out on the Cross, save us!

May 22

Jesus prayed three hours on the Cross; it was really a crucified prayer, without consolation neither inner nor outer. Oh! God, what a great teaching! Pray Jesus to print it in your heart.

— ST. PAUL OF THE CROSS

Heart of Jesus, dwelling of justice and love, have mercy on us!

May 23

Life and death are two significant and decisive elements of Christ's sacrifice. From his smile at Bethlehem, the same smile which lights up the faces of all the children of men when first they appear on earth, to his last gasp and sob on the Cross, which gathered all our sufferings into one to hallow them, and wipe away all our sins by atoning for them, we have seen how Christ lived in this our earthly life.

— POPE ST. JOHN XXIII

From the desire of being extolled, deliver me, Jesus!

May 24

They bound him in the garden, adding chains and ropes, insulting blows and vilest language; for like venomous serpents they shot forth their sacrilegious poison in abuse and blasphemy against him who is adored by angels and men, and who is magnified in heaven and on earth. They left the Garden of Olives in great tumult and uproar, guarding the Savior in their midst. Some of them dragged him along by the ropes in front and others retarded his steps by the ropes hanging from the handcuffs behind. In this manner, with a violence unheard of, they sometimes forced him to fall; at others they jerked him backwards; and then again they pulled him from one side to the other, according to their diabolical whims. Many times they violently threw him to the ground and as his hands were tied behind he fell upon it with his divine countenance and was severely wounded and lacerated. In his falls they pounced upon him, inflicting blows and kicks, trampling upon his body and upon his head and face.

— Venerable Mary of Ágreda

Blood of Christ, help of those in peril, save us!

May 25

Jesus died praying. At the Last Supper he had anticipated his death by giving of himself, thus transforming his death, from within, into an act of love, into a glorification of God.
— POPE BENEDICT XVI

Christ, protect me today against the seduction of vices!

May 26

I do not wish to fly from the cross which God sends me.
— ST. PHILIP NERI

Jesus, grant me the grace to desire that others may be praised and I unnoticed!

May 27

Suffering will never be completely absent from our lives. If we accept it with faith, we are given the opportunity to share the Passion of Jesus and show him our love. One day I went to visit a lady who had terminal cancer. Her pain was tremendous. I told her, "This is nothing but Jesus' kiss, a sign that you are so close to him on the cross that he can kiss you." She joined her hands and said, "Mother, ask Jesus to stop kissing me."

— St. Teresa of Calcutta

From anxiety, sadness, and obsessions, we implore Thee, deliver us, O Lord!

May 28

We need not be surprised, my dear brethren, at the honor which the Church pays to this holy wood, which obtains for us so many graces and as many benefits. We see that the Church makes the Sign of the Cross in all her ceremonies, in the administration of all the Sacraments. Why is this? My friends, this is why. It is because all our prayers and all the Sacraments draw from the Cross their power and their virtue.

— St. John Vianney

O Heart of love, I place all my trust in you!

May 29

There is nothing that consoles me so much, and gives me so much comfort, as afflictions and crosses, and it seems to me that if I had not this support from time to time I should live the most wretched life in the world; and if God should give me the choice whether to go now into paradise or to remain a little longer here to suffer, I should choose the latter rather than the former, for I know how much glory is increased by sufferings.

— St. Catherine of Siena

Lord, grant me the grace to desire that others may be esteemed more than I!

May 30

Again the high priest asked him, "Are you the Christ, the Son of the Blessed?" And Jesus said, **"I am; and you will see the Son of man sitting at the right hand of Power, and coming with the clouds of heaven."** And the high priest tore his clothes, and said, "Why do we still need witnesses? You have heard his blasphemy. What is your decision?" And they all condemned him as deserving death. And some began to spit on him, and to cover his face, and to strike him, saying to him, "Prophesy!" And the guards received him with blows.

— MARK 14:61–65

Heart of Jesus, our peace and reconciliation, have mercy on us!

May 31

I believe that anyone who wishes to be devout and live piously
in Jesus will suffer persecution and will have daily crosses to
carry. But he will never manage to carry a heavy cross, or carry
it joyfully and perseveringly, without a trusting devotion to
Our Lady, who is the very sweetness of the Cross.
— St. Louis de Montfort

*Heart of Jesus, formed by the Holy Spirit in the womb of the
Virgin Mother, have mercy on us!*

JUNE

June 1

I tell you again and again, my brethren, that in the Lord's garden are to be found not only the roses of his martyrs. In it there are also the lilies of the virgins, the ivy of wedding couples, and the violets of widows. On no account may any class of people despair, thinking that God has not called them. Christ suffered for all.

— ST. AUGUSTINE OF HIPPO

O holy Cross, save us!

June 2

Therefore, let us visibly show great faith as we take part in this procession [on the Feast of The Most Holy Body and Blood of Christ; Corpus Christi] and let us say over and over again to ourselves what the prince of the apostles said, "You are Christ, Son of the living God' (Mt 16:16). Let us rouse ourselves to devotion by thoughts of faith and devout reflections such as these: Behold the one who was born of Mary. Behold the body that was in her womb and which she carried in her arms. Behold the flesh that was crucified for me and the blood that was poured out on Calvary.

— BLESSED BASIL MOREAU

Blood of Christ, victor over demons, save us!

June 3

Then he began to invoke a curse on himself and to swear, "I do not know the man." And immediately the cock crowed. And Peter remembered the saying of Jesus, **"Before the cock crows, you will deny me three times."** And he went out and wept bitterly.

— MATTHEW 26:74–75

Lord, grant that I may praise You
with Your saints and with Your angels!

June 4

O ye souls who wish to go on with so much safety and consolation, if you knew how pleasing to God is suffering, and how much it helps in acquiring other good things, you would never seek consolation in anything; but you would rather look upon it as a great happiness to bear the Cross after the Lord.

— ST. JOHN OF THE CROSS

Sinners as we are, we beseech Thee, hear us!

June 5

Lord Jesus, as the hour for which you had come approached, you stood intrepid as one holding the power to lay down your own life and not have someone take it from you. You committed to us not only your body's suffering but also your heart's affection. Your death gave us life, your fear made us brave, your sadness made us joyful, your loathing made us eager, your trouble made us tranquil, and your desolation consoled us.

— St. Bernard of Clairvaux

We adore You, Precious Blood of Jesus Christ!

June 6

A woman with child makes ready for the babe she expects, prepares its cradle, its swaddling clothes and its nurse; even so our Lord, while hanging on his Cross, prepared all that you could need for your happiness, all the means, the graces, the leadings, by which he leads your soul onwards to perfection. Our dear Lord cared for every one of his children as though none other existed.

— St. Francis de Sales

Jesus, most amiable, have mercy on us!

June 7

We want to be Christians — spouses of Jesus — risen and glorified, of course, but without getting too near the Cross.

— BLESSED SOLANUS CASEY

Wisdom of the saints, save us, O holy Cross!

June 8

When diverse temptations overwhelm the soul; when it is steeped in darkness, pain, and spiritual uncertainty; when it hangs on the Cross, bereft of relief and consolation in imitation of Jesus Crucified, but no less, because of God's grace, it peacefully and joyfully accepts the cross and carries and drags it for a very long time — only then is it at the door to true perfection.

— ST. MAXIMILIAN KOLBE

From the desire of being preferred to others, deliver me, Jesus!

June 9

Jesus' Cross is the cathedra, the loftiest ever raised upon the earth. Although Jesus was always a teacher with divine pedagogy, he gradually revealed his heavenly doctrine, and in each mystery of his life he disclosed diverse facets of his unique teaching. In his latter days he imparted to us his final instruction, the loftiest, noblest, and most profound lesson of all, one which constitutes the foundation of his doctrine. This lesson is the one he taught on Calvary; it is the doctrine of the Cross.

— SERVANT OF GOD LUIS MARTINEZ

Jesus, by Thy unjust sentence to death, have mercy on us!

June 10

Those who were marching at the head of the procession tried to push her [Veronica] back; but she made her way through the mob, the soldiers, and the archers, reached Jesus, fell on her knees before him, and presented the veil, saying at the same time, "Permit me to wipe the face of my Lord." Jesus took the veil in his left hand, wiped his bleeding face, and returned it with thanks.

— BLESSED ANNE CATHERINE EMMERICH

Adored be the Holy Face of Jesus!

June 11

I am going to tell you that Jesus Christ, by his sufferings
and his death, has made all our actions meritorious, so
that for the good Christian there is no motion of our
hearts or of our bodies which will not be rewarded if we
perform them for him.
— ST. JOHN VIANNEY

Blessed be the Most Sacred Heart of Jesus!

June 12

**"I came to cast fire upon the earth; and would that it were
already kindled! I have a baptism to be baptized with;
and how I am constrained until it is accomplished!"**
— LUKE 12:49–50

Blood of Christ, strength of martyrs, have mercy on us!

June 13

Truly, there is no sorrow like his sorrow! For those whom he redeemed by so much suffering, he loses so quickly again. His Passion was indeed powerful enough to redeem all men; and yet see how almost all hasten to their damnation! Is there for him a greater sorrow than this? Yet, almost no one seems to care or think of this.

— ST. ANTHONY OF PADUA

Help of the distressed, save us, O holy Cross!

June 14

Indeed, if one thing more than another presents difficulty to the mind and understanding of man, assuredly it is the mystery of the Cross, which beyond all doubt, must be considered the most difficult of all; so much so that only with great difficulty can we grasp the fact that our salvation depends on the Cross, and on him who for us was nailed thereon.

— THE CATECHISM OF THE COUNCIL OF TRENT

You lead us in your triumph. Son of God, deliver us!

June 15

When I entered my solitude, I heard these words: **At the hour of their death, I defend as My own glory every soul that will say this chaplet; or when others say it for a dying person, the indulgence is the same. When this chaplet is said by the bedside of a dying person, God's anger is placated, unfathomable mercy envelops the soul, and the very depths of My tender mercy are moved for the sake of the sorrowful Passion of My Son.**

— St. Faustina Kowalska

Heart of Jesus, obedient to death, have mercy on us!

June 16

He was oppressed, and he was afflicted, yet he opened not his mouth; like a lamb that is led to slaughter, and like a sheep that is before its shearers is silent, so he opened not his mouth.

— Isaiah 53:7

Christ, You took captivity captive. Be our Champion!

June 17

Jesus today has many who would love his heavenly kingdom, but few who carry his Cross; many who yearn for comfort, few who long for distress. Plenty of people he finds to share his banquet, few to share his fast. Everyone desires to take part in his rejoicing, but few are willing to suffer anything for his sake.

— THOMAS À KEMPIS

Christ, have mercy! Lord, have mercy!

June 18

Jesus, the man of sorrows, would like all Christians to imitate him. Jesus has now offered me the chalice again. I accepted it, and this is why he does not spare me from it. My paltry suffering is worth nothing, but in fact it pleases Jesus. Consequently, on certain special days during which he suffered greatly on this earth, he makes me feel his suffering even more intensely. I have been made worthy to suffer with Jesus and like Jesus. Shouldn't this be enough to humble me and cause me to try and hide myself from people's eyes?

— ST. PADRE PIO

Rejoice, O hearts that seek the Lord!

June 19

Jesus continues to live his Passion. He continues to fall, poor and hungry, just like he fell on the way to Calvary. Are we at his side to volunteer to help him? Do we walk next to him with our sacrifice, with our piece of bread — real bread — to help him get over his weakness?

— St. Teresa of Calcutta

From the desire of being approved, deliver me, Jesus!

June 20

The first Christians considered that their greatest happiness was to wear upon themselves this salutary sign of our Redemption. In other times, the women and girls wore a cross which they made their most precious ornament; they hung it around their necks, showing thereby that they were servants of the crucified God. But progressively, as the Faith diminished and as religion became weakened, this sacred sign has become rare or, to be more precise, it has practically disappeared. Notice how the devil works gradually towards evil.

— St. John Vianney

From the snares of the devil, deliver us, O Jesus!

June 21

Whoever aspires to perfection must beware of saying, "I was right. They did that to me without reason." If you are not willing to bear any cross which is not given to you according to reason, perfection is not for you.

— ST. TERESA OF ÁVILA

Jesus, grant me the grace to desire that others may be preferred to me in everything!

June 22

In the Cross of Christ not only is the redemption accomplished through suffering, but also human suffering itself has been redeemed. Christ — without any fault of his own — took on himself "the total evil of sin." The experience of this evil determined the incomparable extent of Christ's suffering, which became the price of the redemption.

— POPE ST. JOHN PAUL II

Heart of Jesus, of infinite majesty, have mercy on us!

June 23

He did nothing that deserved punishment by the Cross
— nothing. But he wished to destroy by his death the
ignominy of the Cross and to render it most glorious by
repairing the damage of the tree [of Eden] on the tree
[of the Cross]. By his Blood, he consecrated it and
rendered it exceedingly noble.

— ST. STANISLAUS PAPCZYŃSKI

Blood of Christ, most worthy of all glory and honor, save us!

June 24

At John's arrival Zechariah's voice is released, and it becomes
clear at the coming of the one who was foretold. The release
of Zachariah's voice at the birth of John is a parallel to the
rending of the veil at Christ's crucifixion.

— ST. AUGUSTINE OF HIPPO

Behold the Lamb of God who takes away the sins of the world!

June 25

I felt that Jesus, in delivering himself up to Divine Justice in satisfaction for the sins of the world, caused his divinity to return, in some sort, into the bosom of the Holy Trinity, consecrated himself, so to speak, in his pure, loving and innocent humanity, and strong only in his ineffable love, gave it up to anguish and suffering. He fell on his face, overwhelmed with unspeakable sorrow, and all the sins of the world displayed themselves before him, under countless forms and in all their real deformity. He took them all upon himself, and in his prayer offered his own adorable Person to the justice of the Heavenly Father, in payment for so awful a debt.

— BLESSED ANNE CATHERINE EMMERICH

Heart of Jesus, in whom dwells the fullness of Divinity, have mercy on us!

June 26

We have just been re-living the drama of Calvary, which
I would dare to describe as the first, the original Mass,
celebrated by Jesus Christ. God the Father delivers his Son
up to death. Jesus, the only Son of God, embraces the Cross
on which they have condemned him to die, and his sacrifice is
accepted by his Father. As a result of that sacrifice, the Holy
Spirit is poured out upon mankind.

— ST. JOSEMARÍA ESCRIVÁ

*Most Sacred Heart of Jesus, may the whole world
burn with love for you!*

June 27

*I saw how they nailed his purest hands, which knew only how to
bless, and his sacred feet, which became fatigued in seeking you.
Then I heard those last words of life, of pardon, of mercy. Amidst
the darkness, when the earth trembled and the trumpets of the
Temple announced the evening sacrifice, I accepted as daughters
and sons all mankind, and especially you.*

— MARY TO BLESSED CONCEPCIÓN CABRERA DE ARMIDA

Jesus, Son of the Virgin Mary, have mercy on us!

June 28

Make a bunch of flowers of Jesus' sufferings, and put it in
your bosom.

— St. Paul of the Cross

Blood of Christ, bringing forth virgins, save us!

June 29

For I delivered to you as of first importance what I also
received, that Christ died for our sins in accordance with the
Scriptures, that he was buried, that he was raised on the third
day in accordance with the Scriptures, and that he appeared
to Cephas, then to the Twelve. Then he appeared to more
than five hundred brethren at one time, most of whom are still
alive, though some have fallen asleep. Then he appeared to
James, then to all the apostles. Last of all, as to one untimely
born, he appeared also to me.

— 1 Corinthians 15:3–8

Saints Peter and Paul, Apostles, pray for us!

June 30

Keep always in your mind, in your mouth, and as a sign the Cross of the Lord in whom you have believed, true God and Son of God. For the Cross of the Lord is your invincible armor against Satan. It is a helm to defend your head, a breastplate to preserve your chest, a buckler to repel the arrows of the evil one, and a sword that will not allow the diabolical tricks and stratagems of the evil power to approach you. By this sign alone has heavenly victory been given to us, and by the Cross has baptism been sanctified.

— St. Martial

Jesus, by the blasphemies uttered against Thee, deliver us!

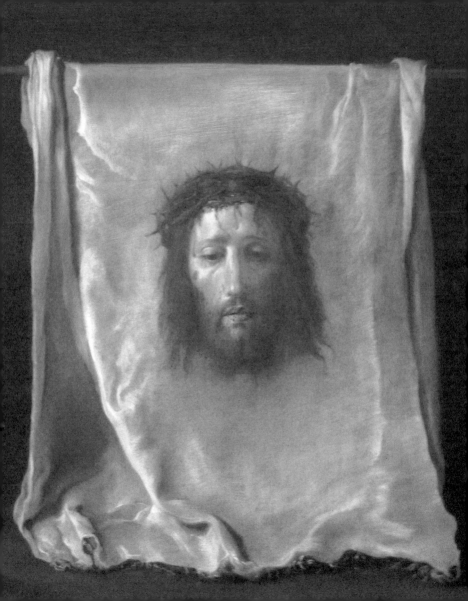

JULY

July 1

Why do angels envy us? Truly, it is for no other reason than that we are able to suffer for our Lord, while they have never suffered anything for him. St. Paul, who was lifted up to heaven amid the joys of paradise, did not count himself blessed except because of his infirmities, and in the Cross of our Lord (2 Cor. 12:3–10; Gal. 6:14).

— St. Francis de Sales

From fear and worry, deliver me, Jesus!

July 2

He suffered death for us all, sinners as we are, and by his example he teaches us that we also have to carry that cross which the flesh and the world lay on the shoulders of those who strive for peace and justice.

— Second Vatican Council (Gaudium Et Spes)

By Thy Sacred Wounds, Jesus, deliver us!

July 3

Follow after Christ and carry your cross for your salvation,
as Christ carried his Cross for your salvation!
— St. Anthony of Padua

Holy Cross, medicine of the sick, save us!

July 4

Had there been no Cross, Christ could not have been
crucified. Had there been no Cross, life itself could not have
been nailed to a tree. And if life had not been nailed to it,
there would be no streams of immortality pouring from
Christ's side, blood and water for the world's cleansing.
— St. Andrew of Crete

Blood of Christ, without which there is no forgiveness, save us!

July 5

Fallen human nature is an abyss of darkness. God knows that, so his mercy always takes pity on our blindness and, in spite of our natural repugnance, offers us, even compels us to receive, the inestimable favor of the Cross. Oh! How happy the divine Master is to hear one single grateful word of appreciation when he offers us a thorn from his crown or a few drops from his bitter chalice! How his Sacred Heart rejoices when the wounded and trusting soul kisses lovingly the precious scourge, the lance, and nails! Oh! If only the gift of God were understood!

— Blessed Dina Bélanger

Jesus, Deliverer, have mercy on us!

July 6

Christ first offered sacrifice here on earth, when he underwent his most bitter death. Then, clothed in the new garment of immortality, with his own blood he entered into the holy of holies, that is, into heaven. There he also displayed before the throne of the heavenly Father that blood of immeasurable price which he had poured out on behalf of all men subject to sin.

— ST. JOHN FISHER

Jesus, by Whose stripes we are healed, have mercy on us!

July 7

Let us be touched at the sight of these sacred wounds, meditating on them often, making ourselves at home with them. Let us go there often, taking refuge in them lovingly in all our temptations.

— BLESSED BASIL MOREAU

Heart of Jesus, desire of the everlasting hills, have mercy on us!

July 8

"Daughters of Jerusalem, do not weep for me, but weep for yourselves and for your children. For behold, the days are coming when they will say, 'Blessed are the barren, and the wombs that never bore, and the breasts that never nursed!' Then they will begin to say to the mountains, 'Fall on us'; and to the hills, 'Cover us.' For if they do this when the wood is green, what will happen when it is dry?"

— LUKE 23:28–31

All you Holy Virgins and Widows, pray for us!

July 9

Only Jesus can comprehend the pain there is for me when I place myself before the sorrowful scene of Calvary. It is incomprehensible that Jesus is comforted not only by sharing his sorrows but also by finding a soul who, out of love for him, asks not for consolation but for participation in his very sufferings. When Jesus wants me to know he loves me, he lets me experience his wounds, his thorns, his agonies.

— ST. PADRE PIO

By Thy own sweet Name, O Lord, deliver us!

July 10

During the three hours of torment I saw him agonizing, and at the end, my child, dying without any support other than the Cross, the nails, and the thorns. The Blood of Jesus had been exhausted; the intensity of my torments knew no limits, when the cruel lance of the centurion pierced his side, piercing the heart whose beats were for all. And I received him in my arms and bathed him with my tears.

— MARY TO BLESSED CONCEPCIÓN CABRERA DE ARMIDA

Passion of Christ, save us!

July 11

The betrayal took place with a kiss. When wickedness would destroy virtue and when man would crucify the Son of God, there is felt a necessity to preface the evil deed by some mark of affection. Judas would complement and deny Divinity with the same lips. Only one word came back in answer to the kiss: "Friend." It was the last time our Lord spoke to Judas.

— VENERABLE FULTON J. SHEEN

May the Holy Cross be my light! Let not the dragon be my guide! Begone, Satan!

July 12

When a soul extols My goodness, Satan trembles before it and flees to the very bottom of hell.

— JESUS TO ST. FAUSTINA KOWALSKA

Heart of Jesus, bruised for our offenses, have mercy on us!

July 13

I will divide him a portion with the great, and he shall divide the spoil with the strong; because he poured out his soul to death and was numbered with the transgressors; yet he bore the sin of many, and made intercession for the transgressors.

— ISAIAH 53:12

You reign forever and ever. Son of God, deliver us!

July 14

Jesus' sufferings must be the jewels of our heart. The sufferings of our Savior are the tokens of his love for us.

— ST. PAUL OF THE CROSS

Heart of Jesus, tabernacle of the Most High, have mercy on us!

July 15

No one can enter by contemplation into the heavenly Jerusalem unless he enters through the blood of the Lamb as through a door.

— St. Bonaventure

Spotless and pure Blood of Jesus, deliver us!

July 16

In the Passion and death of Christ — in the fact that the Father did not spare his own Son, but "for our sake made him sin" — absolute justice is expressed, for Christ undergoes the Passion and Cross because of the sins of humanity. This constitutes a "superabundance" of justice, for the sins of man are "compensated for" by the sacrifice of the Man-God.

— Pope St. John Paul II

Only begotten Son of the eternal Father, save us!

July 17

It was the particular privilege of Christ the Lord to have died when he himself decreed to die, and to have died not so much by external violence as by internal assent. Not only his death, but also its time and place, were ordained by him.

— THE CATECHISM OF THE COUNCIL OF TRENT

Jesus, Son of the living God, have mercy on us!

July 18

His persecutors were surprised to hear that he was dead. How, then, did he die? That agonized, tormented heart, which at the beginning so awfully relieved itself in the rush of blood and the bursting of his pores, at length broke. It broke and he died. It would have broken at once, had he not kept it from breaking. At length the moment came. He gave the word and his heart broke.

— ST. JOHN HENRY NEWMAN

Heart of Jesus, substantially united to the Word of God, have mercy on us!

July 19

By the Cross, we have become children of freedom; by the Cross, Jesus has delivered us from the tyranny of the devil into which sin had led us.

— ST. JOHN VIANNEY

Praise to the Divine Heart that wrought our salvation!

July 20

Often we ask Christ to allow us to share in his sufferings. But when someone is indifferent to us, we forget that then is precisely the moment to share Christ's attitude.

— ST. TERESA OF CALCUTTA

From the desire of being praised, deliver me, Jesus!

July 21

If you are a Joseph of Arimathea, go to the one who ordered his crucifixion, and ask for Christ's body. Make your own the expiation for the sins of the whole world. If you are a Nicodemus, like the man who worshiped God by night, bring spices and prepare Christ's body for burial. If you are one of the Marys, or Salome, or Joanna, weep in the early morning. Be the first to see the stone rolled back, and even the angels, and perhaps Jesus himself.

— St. Gregory Nazianzen

Most Precious Blood of Jesus Christ, save us!

July 22

One day when she [St. Mary Magdalene] asked God to show her a sure way of advancing in his love and of arriving at the height of perfection, he sent St. Michael the Archangel to tell her, on his behalf, that there was no other way for her to arrive at perfection than to meditate on Our Lord's Passion. So he placed a cross in front of her cave and told her to pray before it, contemplating the Sorrowful Mysteries which she had seen take place with her own eyes.

— St. Louis de Montfort

Jesus, raised up on the Cross, have mercy on us!

July 23

When the time of my Son's Passion arrived, his enemies seized him, striking him on his cheek and neck; and spitting upon him, they mocked him. Then, led to the pillar, he stripped himself, and himself stretched his hands to the pillar, which his enemies, piti-less, bound. Now, while tied there he had no clothing, but stood as he was born, and suffered the shame of his nakedness. Then his enemies rose up, for they stood on all sides, his friends having fled, and they scourged his body, pure from all spot or sin. At the first blow, I who stood nearest, fell as if dead, and on recovering my senses I beheld his body bruised and beaten to the very ribs, so that his ribs could be seen; and what was still more bitter, when the scourge was raised, his very flesh was furrowed by the thongs.

— MARY TO ST. BRIDGET OF SWEDEN

Precious Blood of Jesus Christ, Peace of the World, save us!

July 24

The Holy Spirit comes into the soul signed with the precious blood of the Word and of the slain Lamb; or rather that very blood urges it to come, although the Spirit moves in itself and desires to come. You [Holy Spirit] find rest in those creatures who absorb the effects of the blood of the Word and make themselves a worthy dwelling place for you.

— St. Mary Magdalene de Pazzi

God the Holy Spirit, have mercy on us!

July 25

Die, then, to every human sentiment and affliction, that Jesus Christ crucified may live in you, and that being transformed and, as it were, transfigured, you may have no longer feeling in your heart, you may no longer hear nor see any object but your Lord attached to the Cross, and dying for you, following in this example of the Blessed Virgin; so that, being entirely dead to the world, your soul may breathe no other life than that of faith.

— St. Vincent Ferrer

Refuge of sinners, save us!

July 26

The same mercy extended to the one who denied him would be extended to those who would nail him to the Cross and to the penitent thief who would ask for forgiveness. Peter really did not deny that Christ was the Son of God. He denied that he knew "the man," or that he was one of his disciples. But he failed the Master. And yet, knowing all, the Son of God made Peter, who knew sin, and not John, the Rock upon which he built his Church that sinners and the weak might never despair.

— VENERABLE FULTON J. SHEEN

Blood of Christ, solace in sorrow, save us!

July 27

Let us [priests] at least frequently remember what our Redeemer has done and suffered for us. They who frequently remember his Passion give great pleasure to Jesus Christ.

— ST. ALPHONSUS LIGUORI

You are a priest forever, according to the order of Melchizedek!

July 28

The Cross is the crux of the whole matter.
— G.K. CHESTERTON

Jesus, by Thy purple robe of scorn, have mercy on us!

July 29

I, who am spoiler of God's kingdom, well deserve to be
scourged by him!
— ST. LUPUS

*Lord, grant that others become holier than I, provided that
I become as holy as I should!*

July 30

Crosses — the best school wherein to learn appreciation for
the love of Jesus crucified, the divine lover of our souls.
— BLESSED SOLANUS CASEY

With all my being, I love Thee, my Lord!

July 31

Beg a lively contrition for your sins, and a tender love for
Jesus Christ suffering for us. In the Garden of Olives you
have contemplated Jesus Christ making the sacrifice of his
interior consolation. Contemplate him in Jerusalem, making
also sacrifice of all exterior things, which consist of these five
things — his liberty, his friends, his reputation, his happiness,
his own body. In each of these sacrifices consider the Savior as
a victim and as a model; meditate on what he suffers and how
he suffers.

— St. Ignatius of Loyola

Be merciful. Spare us, O Jesus!

AUGUST

August 1

Divinity, on the Cross, was hid; humanity here comes to thought. Believing and confessing both, I seek out what the good thief sought. I see no wounds, as Thomas did, but I profess you God above. Draw me deeply into faith, into your hope, into your love. O memorial of the Lord's sad death, show life to man, O living Bread. Grant that my soul may live through you, by your sweet savor ever fed. Jesus Lord, pelican devout, with your blood my sins dismiss. One single drop could surely save from sin this world's dark edifice.

— St. Thomas Aquinas

Precious Blood of Jesus, Everlasting Covenant, set us free!

August 2

In a very special way, Baptism is related to the Death and Resurrection of Christ. In order to be saved, we have to recapitulate in our own lives the Death and the Resurrection of Christ. What he went through, we have to go through. He is the pattern, and we have to be molded after him. He is the die, we are the coins that have to be stamped with his image.

— VENERABLE FULTON J. SHEEN

From the sins of the flesh, O Lord, deliver us!

August 3

Those who share in Christ's sufferings have before their eyes the Paschal mystery of the Cross and resurrection, in which Christ descends, in a first phase, to the ultimate limits of human weakness and impotence: indeed, he dies nailed to the Cross. But if at the same time in this weakness there is accomplished his lifting up, confirmed by the power of the resurrection, then this means that the weakness of all human sufferings are capable of being infused with the same power of God manifested in Christ's Cross.

— POPE ST. JOHN PAUL II

Strengthen us in our weakness, Almighty God!

August 4

During the Holy Sacrifice of the Mass, which is the greatest, the most solemn, and the most sublime of all those actions which can glorify God, the priest makes the Sign of the Cross over and over again. God desires that we may never lose the memory of it as the surest means to our salvation and the most formidable instrument for repelling the devil. He has created us in the form of a cross so that every man might be the image of this Cross upon which Jesus Christ died to save us.

— St. John Vianney

From all evil, deliver us, O Jesus!

August 5

From the painful bed of the Cross, the new Adam begot us by his word, in the heart of the new Eve, whose virtue produced a new mystery, making Mary truly the mother of all men, past and future.

— Blessed William Joseph Chaminade

Mary, Mother of the Church, pray for us!

August 6

O my great God, you have humbled yourself, you have stooped to take our flesh and blood, and have been lifted up upon the tree! I praise and glorify you ten times more, because you have shown your power by means of your suffering, than had you carried on your work without it. It is worthy of your infinitude thus to surpass and transcend all our thoughts.

— ST. JOHN HENRY NEWMAN

Lord, by Thy perfect submission, deliver us!

August 7

God's compassion for us is all the more wonderful because Christ dies, not for the righteous or the holy but for the wicked and the sinful, and, though the divine nature could not be touched by the sting of death, he took to himself, through his birth as one of us, something he could offer on our behalf.

— ST. LEO THE GREAT

Jesus, judged worthy of death, have mercy on us!

August 8

What the Cross was to Jesus, then, baptism is for us. Jesus Christ was nailed to the Cross to die to his flesh. We are baptized to die to sin, to die to ourselves. On the Cross Jesus Christ had all his senses put to death, so we through baptism should carry the death of Jesus in all our senses.

— St. Padre Pio

Precious Blood of Jesus, Healing Blood, save us!

August 9

Barabbas was freed because of Christ, political freedom though it was. But it was a symbol that through his death men were to be made free. It happened at Passover time when a lamb was substituted for the people and went to death in atonement for their sins. The Savior should suffer and the sinner go free.

— Venerable Fulton J. Sheen

By Your labors, deliver us, O Jesus!

August 10

Christ suffered only for those who follow in his steps, in the sense that Christ's Passion is of no avail to those who do not. The holy martyrs followed Christ even to shedding their life's blood, even to reproducing the very likeness of his Passion.

— ST. AUGUSTINE OF HIPPO

All you holy Martyrs, pray for us!

August 11

Consider the holy humility, the blessed poverty, the untold labors and burdens that he endured for the redemption of the whole human race. Contemplate the ineffable charity that led him to suffer on the wood of the Cross and to die there the most shameful kind of death.

— ST. CLARE OF ASSISI

Bread of the hungry, save us!

August 12

Kiss frequently the crosses which the Lord sends you, and with all your heart, without regarding of what sort they may be; for the more vile and mean they are, the more they deserve their name. The merit of crosses does not consist in their weight, but in the manner in which they are borne. It may show much greater virtue to bear a cross of straw than a very hard and heavy one, because the light ones are also the most hidden and, therefore, least comfortable to our inclination, which always seeks what is showy.

— ST. FRANCIS DE SALES

Jesus, grant me the grace to desire that others may be chosen and I set aside!

August 13

And when evening had come, since it was the day of Preparation, that is the day before the sabbath, Joseph of Arimathea, a respected member of the council, who was also himself looking for the kingdom of God, took courage and went to Pilate, and asked for the body of Jesus. And Pilate wondered if he was already dead. And when he learned from the centurion that he was dead, he granted the body to Joseph. And he brought a linen shroud, and taking him down, wrapped him in the linen shroud, and laid him in a tomb which had been hewn out of rock; and he rolled a stone against the door of the tomb.

— MARK 15:42–46

Jesus, by Thy burial and descent into hell, spare us O Lord!

August 14

And if God should judge it appropriate and, as in the Garden, require that we drink the chalice to the dregs, let us not forget that Jesus not only suffered but also rose in glory. So too we go to the glory of resurrection by way of suffering and the Cross.

— ST. MAXIMILIAN KOLBE

Jesus, most powerful, have mercy on us!

August 15

Mary, the Mother of the living, gives to all her children portions of the Tree of Life, which is the Cross of Jesus. But along with their crosses she also imparts the grace to carry them patiently and even cheerfully; and thus it is that the crosses which she lays upon those who belong to her are rather steeped in sweetness than filled with bitterness.

— St. Louis de Montfort

Blessed be her glorious Assumption!

August 16

The Cross is never to be found in a beautiful room, but at Calvary. Those who want to belong to Jesus have to feel happy to walk with him. No matter how painful it is, we have to share his Passion.

— St. Teresa of Calcutta

From the fear of being humiliated, deliver me, Jesus!

August 17

During the time of the scourging of our Lord, I saw weeping angels approach him many times; I likewise heard the prayers he constantly addressed to his Father for the pardon of our sins — prayers which never ceased during the whole time of the infliction of this cruel punishment.

— BLESSED ANNE CATHERINE EMMERICH

Blood of Christ, shed profusely in the scourging, save us!

August 18

Today, I entered into the bitterness of the Passion of the Lord Jesus. I suffered in a purely spiritual way. I learned how horrible sin was. God gave me to know the whole hideousness of sin. I learned in the depths of my soul how horrible sin was, even the smallest sin, and how much it tormented the soul of Jesus. I would rather suffer a thousand hells than commit even the smallest venial sin.

— ST. FAUSTINA KOWALSKA

From all sin, deliver us, O Jesus.

August 19

In his Passion and death the Son of God, our Savior, intended to atone for and blot out the sins of all ages, to offer for them to his Father a full and abundant satisfaction. Besides, to increase the dignity of this mystery, Christ not only suffered for sinners, but even for those who were the very authors and ministers of all the torments he endured.

— THE CATECHISM OF THE COUNCIL OF TRENT

Jesus, infinite goodness, have mercy on us!

August 20

At the very beginning of my conversion, I made a bouquet of myrrh made up of the sorrows of my Savior. I placed the bouquet upon my heart, thinking of the stripes, the thorns and the nails of his Passion. I used all my mental strength to meditate on these mysteries every day.

— ST. BERNARD OF CLAIRVAUX

Blood of Christ, shed profusely in the scourging, save us!

August 21

When the supreme hour of the Son came, beside the Cross of Jesus there stood Mary his mother, not merely occupied in contemplating the cruel spectacle, but rejoicing that her only Son was offered for the salvation of mankind, and so entirely participating in his Passion, that if it had been possible she would have gladly borne all the torments that her Son bore. And from this community of will and suffering between Christ and Mary she merited to become most worthily the Reparatrix of the lost world and Dispensatrix of all the gifts that our Savior purchased for us by his death and by his blood.

— POPE ST. PIUS X

*Heart of Jesus, House of God and Gate of Heaven,
have mercy on us!*

August 22

During Holy Mass, I saw the Lord Jesus nailed upon the Cross amidst great torments. A soft moan issued from his Heart. After some time, he said, **I thirst. I thirst for the salvation of souls. Help me, my daughter, to save souls. Join your sufferings to my Passion and offer them to the heavenly Father for sinners.**

— JESUS TO ST. FAUSTINA KOWALSKA

By your Cross and Resurrection, deliver us, O Jesus!

August 23

"Are you the only visitor to Jerusalem who does not know the things that have happened there in these days?" And he said to them, "**What things?**" And they said to him, "Concerning Jesus of Nazareth, who was a prophet mighty in deed and word before God and all the people, and how our chief priests and rules delivered him up to be condemned to death, and crucified him."

— LUKE 24:18–21

That we may take up our cross daily and follow Thee, we beseech Thee, hear us, O Lord!

August 24

Jesus fled, when the people desired to choose our Savior as king, as they had been fed by him to satiety. Indeed, he was alone in solitude. Now, however, he rejoices to be crowned with thorns, and to take up the scepter of reeds, and "love sustained him in his intense zeal for new punishments."
So that to each sinner who approaches him as a beggar, he stretches out this scepter of reeds as a sign of clemency, and accepts him completely absolved by grace.
— ST. STANISLAUS PAPCZYŃSKI

Blood of Christ, hope of the penitent, save us!

August 25

The days of the Passion are the days when even the stones cry. What for? The High Priest has died, won't you cry?
— ST. PAUL OF THE CROSS

Precious Blood of the Son of God, save us!

August 26

I am not so much astonished at the injustice of Pilate in condemning Jesus, but what touches me is to see Jesus Christ submitting to so unjust a sentence; to see him taking up his Cross with such wonderful humility, meekness, and resignation; to look at him on Calvary allowing himself to be stripped and stretched upon the Cross, offering his hands and feet to be nailed and offering himself to his Father as he alone could. This makes me love the Cross; without it I do not think I could be happy.

— St. Claude de la Colombière

Reward of the just, save us, O holy Cross!

August 27

On Sunday when I was looking at a picture of our Lord on the Cross, I saw the blood coming from one of his hands, and I felt terribly sad to think that it was falling to the earth and that no one was rushing forward to catch it. I determined to stay continually at the foot of the Cross to receive it. I knew that I should have to spread it among other souls.

— St. Thérèse of Lisieux

Holy Cross on which the Lamb of God was offered, save us!

August 28

The death of the Lord our God should not be a cause of shame for us; rather it should be our greatest hope, our greatest glory. In taking upon himself the death that he found in us, he has most faithfully promised to give us life in him, such as we cannot have of ourselves. He loved us so much that, sinless, he suffered for us sinners the punishment we deserved for our sins.

— St. Augustine of Hippo

You rule with a rod of iron. Son of God, deliver us!

August 29

Therefore, because John [the Baptist] shed his blood for the truth, he surely died for Christ. Through his birth, preaching and baptizing, he bore witness to the coming birth, preaching and baptism of Christ, and by his own suffering he showed that Christ also would suffer.

— St. Bede the Venerable

St. John the Baptist, pray for us!

August 30

Our Lord used many pulpits during his public life, such as Peter's bark pushed into the sea, the mountaintop, the streets of Tyre and Sidon, the temple, the country road near a cemetery, and a banquet hall. But all faded into insignificance compared to the pulpit of the Cross.

— VENERABLE FULTON J. SHEEN

Most Sacred Heart of Jesus, may the whole world burn with love for you!

August 31

Jesus loved profoundly his interior suffering, relinquishing it only with his last breath. His suffering is immortal, preserved in loving souls. He will choose the most select souls to guard the sacred fire of his suffering.

— SERVANT OF GOD LUIS MARTINEZ

You must reign until you have put all your enemies under your feet. Son of God, deliver us!

SEPTEMBER

September 1

Now the chief priests and the elders persuaded the people to ask for Barabbas and destroy Jesus. The governor asked again and said to them, "Which of the two do you want me to release for you?" And they said, "Barabbas." Pilate said to them, "Then what shall I do with Jesus who is called Christ?" They all said, "Let him be crucified." And he said, "Why, what evil has he done?" But they shouted all the more, "Let him be crucified."

— MATTHEW 27:20–23

Innocent Jesus, scourged at the pillar, have mercy on us!

September 2

Pharisaism and Sadduceeism, which were enemies, united in the Crucifixion. The Cross of Christ unites his friends — that is obvious; but the Cross also unites his enemies. The worldly always drop their lesser hates in the face of the hatred of the Divine. It was a good joke, this prisoner covered with his own blood, hated by his own people, claiming to be a king. Herod could trust Pilate to see the humor of it. When Pilate and he would laugh over it together, they would no longer be enemies — even when the butt of the humor was God. The only time laughter is wicked is when it is turned against him who gave it.

— VENERABLE FULTON J. SHEEN

Blood of Christ, incarnate Word of God, save us!

September 3

Christ suffered without sin on his hands, for he committed no sin and deceit was not found on his lips. Yet he suffered the pain of the Cross for our redemption. His prayer to God was pure, his alone out of mankind, for in the midst of his suffering he prayed for his persecutors: **Father, forgive them, for they do not know what they are doing**.
— St. Gregory the Great

Jesus, laden with the Cross and led to Calvary, have mercy on us!

September 4

Our Lord continues to show me in spirit the millions of souls that, during his agony, he saw falling into hell. And he is there, praying and suffering, surrounded by only a small number of souls. What a moving sight!
— Blessed Dina Bélanger

For those who are indifferent to your sufferings, O Lord, have mercy!

September 5

In his Passion Jesus taught us how to forgive out of love, how to forget out of humility. So let us at the beginning of the Passion of Christ examine our hearts fully and see if there is any unforgiving hurt, and unforgotten bitterness.

— ST. TERESA OF CALCUTTA

Jesus, friend of the poor, have mercy on us!

September 6

Our high priest is Christ Jesus, our sacrifice is his precious body which he immolated on the altar of the Cross for the salvation of all men. The blood that was poured out for our redemption was not that of goats or calves (as in the old law) but that of the most innocent lamb, Christ Jesus our Savior. The temple in which our high priest offered sacrifice was not made by hands but built by the power of God alone. For he shed his blood in the sight of the world, a temple fashioned by the hand of God alone.

— ST. JOHN FISHER

Jesus, hated without cause, have mercy on us!

September 7

Meditation on my Passion will help you rise above all things. By meditating on my Passion, your soul acquires a distinct beauty.

— JESUS TO ST. FAUSTINA KOWALSKA

Christ, your Cross disarmed and triumphed over the principalities and powers. You are our champion!

September 8

The Blessed Virgin Mary was ever united to her Divine Son by interior spiritual communications; she was, therefore, fully aware of all that happened to him — she suffered with him, and joined in his continual prayer for his murderers.

— BLESSED ANNE CATHERINE EMMERICH

Blessed be the great Mother of God, Mary most holy!

September 9

All of our works should be done with the Sign of the Cross.
— ST. AMBROSE

Holy Trinity, one God, have mercy on us!

September 10

In foretelling his Passion, the Savior wished to arouse in the Apostles a feeling of trust in the Divine Mercy.
— BLESSED MICHAEL SOPOĆKO

Sacred Heart of Jesus, protect our families!

September 11

That Christ our Lord suffered the most excruciating torments of mind and body is certain. In the first place, there was no part of his body that did not experience the most agonizing torture. His hands and feet were fastened with nails to the Cross; his head was pierced with thorns and smitten with a reed; his face was befouled with spittle and buffeted with blows; his whole body was covered with stripes.

— THE CATECHISM OF THE COUNCIL OF TRENT

Christ, You came to destroy the works of the devil. Set us free!

September 12

During her whole life the Blessed Mother's chief concern was meditation on the virtues and sufferings of her Son. After our Lord's Ascension our Blessed Lady spent the rest of her life in visiting the places that had been hallowed by his presence and sufferings. When she was in those places she used to meditate upon his boundless love and upon his terrible Passion.

— ST. LOUIS DE MONTFORT

Blessed be the name of Mary, Virgin and Mother!

September 13

If sufferings had no other reward than being able to bear something for that God who loves you, is not this a great reward and a sufficient remuneration? Whoever loves, understands what I say.

— St. John Chrysostom

O Sacred Heart of Jesus, burning with love for mankind, have mercy of us!

September 14

The Cross is honorable because it is both the sign of God's suffering and the trophy of his victory. It stands for his suffering because on it he freely suffered death. But it is also his trophy because it was the means by which the devil was wounded and death conquered; the barred gates of hell were smashed, and the Cross became the one common salvation of the whole world.

— St. Andrew of Crete

Heart of Jesus, victim for our sins, have mercy on us!

September 15

Our Savior climbs to Calvary, and his holy mother climbs there with him. He is raised up on the Cross. Can you see her standing there at the foot of this instrument of torture, her hands folded, her eyes fixed on her dying son, unable to take them off his body covered with wounds, off the thorns crowning his head, off the nails piercing his feet and his hands, off his eyes drooping with death, off his mouth slightly opened to let sound the words of his last wishes, off the wound made in his side by the lance? All this for three hours already! Queen of martyrs, I throw myself at your feet to ask your pardon for having thus martyred you by my sins. I beg you to obtain pardon for me from your divine son by granting me your own pardon.

— BLESSED BASIL MOREAU

Jesus, strength of martyrs, have mercy on us!

September 16

We glory in the Cross of the Lord, the power of which perfects all of the sacraments, without the sign of which nothing is holy, nor is any consecration effectual.

— ST. CYPRIAN

Heart of Jesus, source of all consolation, have mercy on us!

September 17

Sorrow does not come first, then look at the Cross; rather sorrow for sins springs from a vision of the Cross. All excuses are cast aside when the vileness of sin is most poignantly revealed. But the arrow of sin that wounds and crucifies brings the balm of forgiveness that heals.

— VENERABLE FULTON J. SHEEN

Glorious King of Heaven and earth, save us!

September 18

My God, I know well, you could have saved us at your word, without yourself suffering; but you chose to purchase us at the price of your Blood. I look on you, the Victim lifted up on Calvary, and I know and protest that your death was an expiation for the sins of the whole world. I believe and know, that you alone could have offered a meritorious atonement; for it was your Divine Nature which gave your sufferings worth.

— St. John Henry Newman

Precious Blood of Jesus, Healing Blood, set us free!

September 19

Jesus made up for the disobedience which is always included in human sin, by satisfying on our behalf the demands of divine justice. Many saints are "heroes of the Cross." In the work of salvation accomplished in the Passion and death on the Cross, Jesus pushed to the very limit the manifestation of the divine love for humanity, which is at the origin of his oblation and of the Father's plan.

— Pope St. John Paul II

Jesus, Divine Mercy Incarnate, heal us!

September 20

True reverence for the Lord's Passion means fixing the eyes of our heart on Jesus crucified and recognizing in him our own humanity. The earth — our earthly nature — should tremble at the suffering of its Redeemer. The rocks — the hearts of unbelievers — should burst asunder.

— St. Leo the Great

Jesus, obedient unto death, save us!

September 21

Now from the sixth hour there was darkness over all the land until the ninth hour. And about the ninth hour Jesus cried with a loud voice, **"Eli, Eli, lama sabach-thani?"** that is **"My God, my God, why have you forsaken me?"**

— Matthew 27:45–46

Saint Matthew, Apostle and Evangelist, pray for us!

September 22

Oh how fully did he pay the debt of sin! Oh how well he paid the Creditor in ready money upon the table of the Cross! How many whips and stripes, how many punctures and wounds, how many injuries, tears, torments, and at last, cruelest death!

— ST. THOMAS OF VILLANOVA

To You all authority in Heaven and on earth has been given. We love you, Jesus!

September 23

We don't reach salvation without the stormy sea, continually threatened with disaster. Calvary is the hill of the saints, but from there we pass on to another mountain [heaven].

— ST. PADRE PIO

Jesus, our way and our life, have mercy on us!

September 24

The Passion of Jesus Christ is the shortest way to perfection.
Jesus' life was nothing but a Cross.
— ST. PAUL OF THE CROSS

My Jesus, loaded with contempt, cleanse me of my sins by your Precious Blood!

September 25

Just before the murder he prayed for all the murderous race of men, saying **"They know not what they do"**; is there anything to say to that? Is there any need to repeat and spin out the story of how the tragedy trailed up the Via Dolorosa and how they threw him in haphazard with two thieves in one of the ordinary batches of execution; and how in all that horror and howling wilderness of desertion one voice spoke in homage, a startling voice from the very last place where it was looked for, the gibbet of the criminal; and he said to that nameless ruffian, **"This night shalt thou be with me in Paradise"**? Is there anything to put after that but a full-stop?
— G.K. CHESTERTON

Lord of all, we bow before Thee!

September 26

Are you forgetting that at your Baptism you accepted the Cross, which you must never abandon until death, and that it is the key that you will use to open the door to Heaven? Are you forgetting the words of our Savior: **"If any man will come after me, let him deny himself, take up his cross daily, and follow me**." Not for a day, not for a week, not for a year, but all our lives. The saints had a great fear of passing any time without suffering, for they looked upon it as time lost.

— ST. JOHN VIANNEY

To you, O Lord, be glory and honor forever and ever!

September 27

We have never so much cause for consolation, as when we find ourselves oppressed by sufferings and trials; for these make us like Christ our Lord, and this resemblance is the true mark of our predestination.

— ST. VINCENT DE PAUL

Most Sweet Jesus, Redeemer of the human race, look down upon us, humbly prostrate before You!

September 28

If God causes you to suffer much, it is a sign that he has great designs for you, and that he certainly intends to make you a saint. And if you wish to become a great saint, entreat him yourself to give you much opportunity for suffering; for there is no wood better to kindle the fire of holy love than the wood of the Cross, which Christ used for his own great sacrifice of boundless charity.

— St. Ignatius of Loyola

Lift high the Cross, the love of Christ proclaim!

September 29

As long as we are on this earth, we will always feel a natural aversion to suffering. It is a chain that accompanies us everywhere we go. You can be certain, however, that even if our disposition is to desire the Cross and we willingly embrace it and submit to it out of love for God, that does not mean we will stop feeling nature's demands in our flesh to not want to suffer. Who most loved the Cross of the divine Master? Well, even he, in his most holy humanity during his freely chosen agony, prayed that the chalice be removed from him if possible.

— ST. PADRE PIO

Precious Blood of Jesus Christ, purify us!

September 30

In mediating on Jesus being taken prisoner in the Garden,
two things touched me very much and occupied my thoughts:
first, the way Christ went forward to meet those who had
come to apprehend him: his firmness, courage, and peace just
as if his soul had been steeped in calm. The second thing that
struck me was our Lord's dispositions with regards to Judas,
who betrayed him, to the apostle, who abandoned him, and to
the priests and others who were the cause of the persecution
he suffered. Amidst it all, Jesus remained perfectly calm; his
love for his disciples and enemies was not altered at all; he
grieved over the harm they did themselves.

— ST. CLAUDE DE LA COLOMBIÈRE

Support of the weak, save us.

OCTOBER

October 1

I long to be a martyr. From my childhood I have dreamt of martyrdom, and it is a dream which has grown more and more real in my little cell in Carmel. But I don't want to suffer just one torment. I should have to suffer them all to be satisfied. Like you, my adorable Jesus, I want to be scourged and crucified. I want to be flayed like St. Bartholomew. Like St. John, I want to be flung into boiling oil. Like St. Ignatius of Antioch, I long to be ground by the teeth of wild beasts, ground into a bread worthy of God. With St. Agnes and St. Cecilia, I want to offer my neck to the sword of the executioner and, like Joan of Arc, murmur the name of Jesus at the stake. My heart leaps when I think of the unheard tortures Christians will suffer in the reign of anti-Christ. I want to endure them all.

— St. Thérèse of Lisieux

Jesus, King of martyrs, thank You for dying for us!

October 2

If we were to ask him [Moses] what he meant, and how the blood of an irrational beast could possibly save men endowed with reason, his answer would be that the saving power lies not in the blood itself, but in the fact that it is a sign of the Lord's blood. In those days, when the destroying angel saw the blood on the doors he did not dare to enter, so how much less will the devil approach now when he sees, not that figurative blood on the doors, but the true blood on the lips of believers, the doors of the temple of Christ.

— ST. JOHN CHRYSOSTOM

From the fear of being despised, deliver me, Jesus!

October 3

Our Lord looked forward to giving his life as a ransom for sin; he had described himself as having a baptism wherewith he was to be baptized. John gave him the baptism of water, but the Roman soldiers now gave him his baptism of blood. After opening his sacred flesh with violent stripes, they now put on him a purple robe which adhered to his bleeding body. Then they plaited a crown of thorns which they placed on his head. How the soldiers cursed when one thorn plucked their fingers, but how they sneered when the crown of thorns crowned his brow! They then mocked him and put a reed in his hand after beating him on the head. Then they knelt down before him in feigned adoration.

— Venerable Fulton J. Sheen

Son of God, Your robe is dipped in Blood, deliver us!

October 4

I thank thee, O Lord, my God, for these my pains, and I beseech thee, O Lord, to increase them a hundredfold, for this shall be most acceptable to me, that thou spare not to afflict me with suffering, because the fulfillment of thy Holy Will is to me an overflowing consolation.

— St. Francis of Assisi

With all my heart, soul, and mind, I love Thee, my God!

October 5

O Jesus, when I consider the great price of Your Blood, I rejoice at its immensity, for one drop alone would have been enough for the salvation of all sinners. Although sin is an abyss of wickedness and ingratitude, the price paid for us can never be equaled. Therefore, let every soul trust in the Passion of the Lord, and place its hope in His mercy. God will not deny His mercy to anyone. Heaven and earth may change, but God's mercy will never be exhausted.

— St. Faustina Kowalska

Jesus, merciful and full of love, heal us!

October 6

I believe that the same Son of God was conceived among men, a true man with no sin. I believe the same Son of God was captured by the hatred of some of the Jews who did not believe, was bound unjustly, covered with spittle, and scourged.

— ST. BRUNO

Refuge of sinners, save us.

October 7

What are the thoughts of the angels and saints, and what are my thoughts in beholding this world and all the faithful in such a dangerous and dreadful state of carelessness, when they have the Passion and Death of my divine Son before their eyes, and when they have me, for their mother and intercessor, and his most pure life and mine for an example?

— MARY TO VENERABLE MARY OF ÁGREDA

Our Lady of the Rosary, pray for us!

October 8

Before beginning your work, my dear brethren, never fail to make the Sign of the Cross.
— St. John Vianney

By Thy most profound humility, O Lord, deliver us!

October 9

His bodily pains were greater than those of any martyr, because he willed them to be greater.
— St. John Henry Newman

Heart of Jesus, delight of all the saints, have mercy on us!

October 10

Saint Paul tells us that "those who belong to Christ Jesus have crucified the flesh with its passions and desires' [Galatians 5:24]. It seems from this teaching that whoever wants to be a true Christian, that is, one who lives in the spirit of Jesus Christ, must mortify the flesh for no other reason than devotion to Jesus — who for love of us chose to mortify his limbs on the Cross. You need to dominate the flesh, to crucify it, because the flesh is the root of all evils.

— St. Padre Pio

Holy Wisdom of God, teach me!

October 11

There is a great lesson here for us all. We may not be called to endure a cruel martyrdom, but we are called to the exercise of constant discipline and the daily mortification of our passions. This way, a real "Way of the Cross," our daily, unavoidable and indispensable duty, which at times becomes more heroic in its requirements, leads us step by step towards a more and more perfect resemblance with Jesus Christ, and a share in his merits and in the atonement through his innocent blood for every sin in us and in all people.

— POPE ST. JOHN XXIII

Blood of Christ, inebriate me!

October 12

Consider that Christ's humanity truly acquired omnipotence and obtained power over all creation after he was lifted up on the Cross and put to death by unheard of torments. Learn this: the graver are the crosses that you endure on earth, the greater shall be the rewards that await you in Heaven.

— ST. STANISLAUS PAPCZYŃSKI

Raise our minds to desire the things of Heaven, Lord!

October 13

Grace of the mystery of the Death and Passion of our Lord and Savior Jesus Christ, come down into my soul and make me truly holy.

— ST. LOUIS DE MONTFORT

May we may perfectly know and love the Crucified.

October 14

In the Passion alone we have the most illustrious example of the exercise of every virtue. For he so displayed patience, humility, exalted charity, meekness, obedience and unshaken firmness of soul, not only in suffering for justice's sake, but also in meeting death, that we may truly say on the day of his Passion alone, our Savior offered, in his own Passion, a living exemplification of all the moral precepts inculcated during the entire time of his public ministry.

— THE CATECHISM OF THE COUNCIL OF TRENT

Jesus, example of virtues, have mercy on us!

October 15

When I think in how many ways the Lord suffered, and that for no fault of his own, I do not know of what I was thinking when I complained of my sufferings and tried to escape from them.

— St. Teresa of Ávila

Thou who savest by Thy grace, we beseech Thee hear us!

October 16

Behold this Heart which has loved men so much that it spared no sacrifice, not even death and annihilation, in order to testify to them its love. And in return I receive from the greater part of mankind only ingratitude, by reason of the contempt, irreverence, sacrilege and coldness which they show me in this Sacrament of Love.

— Jesus to St. Margaret Mary Alacoque

Jesus, meek and humble of Heart,
make our hearts like unto Thine!

October 17

I prefer death in Christ Jesus to power over the farthest limits of the earth. He who died in place of us is the one object of my quest. He who rose for our sakes is my one desire. The time for my birth is close at hand. Forgive me, my brothers. Do not stand in the way of my birth to real life; do not wish me stillborn. My desire is to belong to God. Do not, then, hand me back to the world. Do not try to tempt me with material things. Let me attain pure light. Only on my arrival there can I be fully a man. Give me the privilege of imitating the Passion of my God.

— St. Ignatius of Antioch

O holy Cross, save us!

October 18

Two others also, who were criminals, were led away to be put to death with him. And when they came to the place which is called The Skull, there they crucified him, and the criminals, one on the right and one on the left. And Jesus said, **"Father, forgive them; for they know not what they do."** And they cast lots to divide his garments.

— LUKE 23:32–34

Saint Luke the Evangelist, pray for us!

October 19

Jesus, my Lord and Savior, what can I give you in return for
all the favors you have first conferred on me? I will take from
your hand the cup of your sufferings and call on your name.
I vow before your eternal Father and the Holy Spirit, before
your most holy Mother and her most chaste spouse, before the
angels, apostles and martyrs, before my blessed fathers Saint
Ignatius and Saint Francis Xavier — in truth I vow to you, Jesus
my Savior, that as far as I have the strength I will never fail to
accept the grace of martyrdom, if some day you in your infinite
mercy should offer it to me, your most unworthy servant.

— ST. JOHN DE BRÉBEUF

Jesus, High Priest, save us!

October 20

It is very good and holy to consider the Passion of our Lord and to meditate on it, for by this sacred path we reach union with God. In this most holy school we learn true wisdom, for it was there that all the saints learned it. Indeed when the Cross of our dear Jesus has planted its roots more deeply in your hearts, then will you rejoice.

— ST. PAUL OF THE CROSS

Your eyes are like a flame of fire. Son of God, deliver us!

October 21

The Last Judgment was prefigured on Calvary: the Judge was in the center, and the two divisions of humanity on either side. When he comes in glory to judge all men, the Cross will be with him then too, but as a badge of honor, not shame.

— VENERABLE FULTON J. SHEEN

Thy Kingdom come!

October 22

The events of Good Friday and, even before that, in prayer in Gethsemane, introduce a fundamental change into the whole course of the revelation of love and mercy in the messianic mission of Christ. The one who "went about doing good and healing" and "curing every disease" now himself seems to merit the greatest mercy and to appeal for mercy, when he is arrested, abused, condemned, scourged, crowned with thorns, when he is nailed to the Cross and dies amidst agonizing torments.

— POPE ST. JOHN PAUL II

Pope St. John Paul II, apostle of Divine Mercy, pray for us!

October 23

How happy are the souls that are wounded by our Savior's sufferings and always carry them fixed in their heart with a painful and loving memory!

— ST. PAUL OF THE CROSS

Heart of Jesus, of Whose fullness we have all received, have mercy on us!

October 24

God gave the martyrs his special assistance, but this very same God abandoned Jesus, the man of sorrows, in the midst of his sufferings and great pain. Christ's body was far more delicate than ours and hence felt pain more than we do. Well then, who can even imagine what Jesus suffered? His whole life passed before him. How much he must have suffered out of love for us. Such an intense and prolonged agony!

— St. Anthony Mary Claret

Heart of Jesus, hope of all who die in You, have mercy on us!

October 25

No one, however weak, is denied a share in the victory of the Cross. No one is beyond the help of the prayer of Christ. His prayer brought benefit to the multitude that raged against him. How much more does it bring to those who turn to him in repentance.

— St. Leo the Great

By Thy buffetings and stripes, Jesus, deliver us!

October 26

If our interior crosses are so numerous and if the public crosses, these images of that Cross on which our God died, are also so numerous, it is that we may have always present in our thoughts the reminder that we are the children of a crucified God.

— St. John Vianney

Lord, take our hearts and make us messengers of love to the world!

October 27

The Cross is my sure salvation; the Cross I ever adore; the Cross of my Lord is with me; the Cross is my sure refuge.

— St. Thomas Aquinas

In the name of the Father, and of the Son, and of the Holy Spirit. Amen!

October 28

"Put your sword back into its place; for all who take the sword will perish by the sword. Do you think that I cannot appeal to my Father, and he will at once send me more than twelve legions of angels? But how then should the Scriptures be fulfilled, that it must be so?"

— MATTHEW 26:52–54

Lord, from the malicious enemy, defend me!

October 29

You are my Creator, eternal Trinity, and I am your creature. You have made of me a new creation in the blood of your Son, and I know that you are moved with love at the beauty of your creation, for you have enlightened me.

— ST. CATHERINE OF SIENA

Heart of Jesus, obedient even to death, have mercy on us!

October 30

The love of our Lord's Heart was in no way diminished by the treason of Judas, the flight of the apostles, and the persecution of his enemies. Jesus was only grieved at the harm they did themselves; his sufferings helped to assuage his grief because he saw in them a remedy for the sins committed by his enemies.

— St. Claude de la Colombière

Jesus, sold for thirty pieces of silver, have mercy on us!

October 31

This blood, if rightly received, drives away demons and keeps them far away from us. For wherever they see the Lord's blood, demons flee and angels run to gather together. For this blood, poured forth, washed clean all the world.

— St. John Chrysostom

Sacred Blood of Jesus, deliver us!

NOVEMBER

November 1

"Worthy is the Lamb who was slain, to receive power and wealth and wisdom and might and honor and glory and blessing!"

— REVELATION 5:12

Lamb of God, who takes away the sins of the world, have mercy on us!

November 2

And Pilate asked him, "Are you the King of the Jews?" And he answered him, **"You have said so."** And the chief priests accused him of many things. And Pilate again asked him, "Have you no answer to make? See how many charges they bring against you." But Jesus made no further answer, so that Pilate wondered.

— MARK 15:2–5

Jesus, you are the Way, the Truth, and the Life!

November 3

As the darkness continued to grow more and more dense, the silence became perfectly astounding; everyone appeared terror-struck; some looked at the sky, while others, filled with remorse, turned toward the Cross, smote their breasts, and were converted. The thick fog penetrated everything. Stillness reigned around the Cross. Jesus hung upon it alone; forsaken.

— BLESSED ANNE CATHERINE EMMERICH

Lamb of God, who takest away the sins of the world, spare us, O Lord!

November 4

Our Lord often thought of his Passion and death, spoke of it with courage, and went unfalteringly towards it. It was the continual act of his sacrifice for us, of submission to the will of his Heavenly Father, and of his infinite mercy towards us.

— BLESSED MICHAEL SOPOĆKO

Sweet Heart of Jesus, be my love!

NOVEMBER

November 5

Christ through his own salvific suffering is very much present in every human suffering, and can act from within that suffering by the powers of his Spirit of truth, his consoling Spirit. This is not all: the Divine Redeemer wishes to penetrate the soul of every sufferer through the heart of his holy mother, the first and most exalted of all the redeemed.

— POPE ST. JOHN PAUL II

May the Lord bless us, protect us from all evil,
and bring us to everlasting life. Amen!

November 6

"Have you come out as against a robber, with swords and clubs to capture me? Day after day I sat in the temple teaching, and you did not seize me. But all this has taken place, that the Scriptures of the prophets might be fulfilled." Then all the disciples deserted him and fled.

— MATTHEW 26:55–56

Lord, bid me come unto You!

November 7

His own sufferings, far from troubling him, comforted him because he knew they would act as a remedy for the sins of his enemies. His Heart was without bitterness and full of tenderness toward his enemies in spite of their perfidy and of all they made him suffer.

— St. Claude de la Colombière

Heart of Jesus, our life and Resurrection, have mercy on us!

November 8

God has made me understand in his light what a treasure suffering is, and we will never understand enough the extent to which he loves us when he gives us trials; the Cross is a token of his love!

— Blessed Elizabeth of the Trinity

Precious Blood of Jesus, greater than the heavens, save us!

November 9

God has suffered so much for me! Is it too much if I do something for his love? Every now and then you should remember our Savior's sufferings.

— St. Paul of the Cross

Blood of Christ, freeing souls from Purgatory, save us!

November 10

Existing before time began, he began to exist at a moment in time. Lord of the universe, he hid his infinite glory and took the nature of a servant. Incapable of suffering as God, he did not refuse to be a man, capable of suffering. Immortal, he chose to be subject to the laws of death.

— St. Leo the Great

Jesus Christ, King of the Universe, have mercy on us!

November 11

As God took a rib from Adam's side to fashion a woman, so Christ has given us blood and water from his side to fashion the Church. God took the rib when Adam was in a deep sleep, and in the same way Christ gave us the blood and water after his own death.

— ST. JOHN CHRYSOSTOM

Water from Christ's side, wash me!

November 12

We have died with Christ. We carry about in our bodies the sign of his death, so that the living Christ may also be revealed in us. The life we live is not now our ordinary life but the life of Christ: a life of sinlessness, of chastity, of simplicity and every other virtue.

— ST. AMBROSE

Jesus, spat upon, blindfolded, and struck with blows, have mercy on us!

November 13

From his open wounds, from his lacerated breast, from the extreme suffering of his soul, from the holy efficacy of his blood, there issued forth the life, the truth, the eternal. When Jesus was raised on high, he drew all men to himself. When his side was opened there issued forth the pure, immaculate, holy, fertile and immortal Church, as Eve had mysteriously come from the side of Adam.

— SERVANT OF GOD LUIS MARTINEZ

Jesus, Redeemer of the world, have mercy on us!

November 14

Eternal Father, turn Your merciful gaze upon all mankind and especially upon poor sinners, all enfolded in the Most Compassionate Heart of Jesus. For the sake of His sorrowful Passion, show us Your mercy, that we may praise the omnipotence of Your mercy forever and ever. Amen.

— ST. FAUSTINA KOWALSKA

Jesus, I trust in You!

November 15

There is no one who so deeply realizes what Christ went through as the man who has had to suffer as he did. The Cross, then, is at all times ready for you; never a place on earth but you will find it awaiting you. Dash off here or there, you can't get away from it.

— THOMAS À KEMPIS

By Your death and burial, deliver us, O Jesus!

November 16

My daughter, you will never be able to do me a greater service at any time than bearing patiently, in honor of my Passion, whatever tribulation may come to you, whether it be interior or exterior, always forcing yourself to do all those things that are most contrary to your desires.

— JESUS TO ST. GERTRUDE

Jesus, grant me the grace to desire that others may be loved more than I!

November 17

Beloved, do not be surprised at the fiery ordeal which comes upon you to prove you, as though something strange were happening to you. But rejoice in so far as you share Christ's sufferings, that you may also rejoice and be glad when his glory is revealed. If you are reproached for the name of Christ, you are blessed, because the spirit of glory and of God rests upon you.

— I PETER 4:12–14

Jesus, son of Mary and Joseph, have mercy on us!

November 18

Each thing has its season: in one we press grapes, and in another we bring the vintage forth from the cellar, but we must press, and do so carefully and without anxiety. On the Cross, there is but one grape, although it is worth more than thousands. How much nourishment have holy souls found there, by thinking upon grace and virtues that our Savior showed forth to the world. Make a good harvest of your earthly labors, and they will serve you as a ladder to climb to spiritual ones.

— St. Francis de Sales

By Thy crown of thorns, have mercy on us!

November 19

Ah! How great a misery is it that I have lifted up my hand against God. How could I ever fancy he would forgive me! Unless he had himself told us that he underwent his bitter Passion in order that he might forgive us. I acknowledge, O Jesus, in the anguish and agony of my heart, that my sins it was that struck thee on the face, that bruised thy sacred arms, that tore thy flesh with iron rods, that nailed thee to the Cross, and let thee slowly die upon it.

— St. John Henry Newman

We adore Thee, O Christ, and we praise Thee!

November 20

The Lord during his Passion had no greater joy than to see in the soul of his most blessed mother, the beautiful likeness of himself and the full fruits of his Passion and death. This joy, to a certain extent, comforted Christ our Lord also in that hour.

— Venerable Mary of Ágreda

Sacred Heart of Jesus, I have confidence in Thee!

November 21

The Heart of Jesus and the Heart of Mary were made one on Calvary in this obedience to the Father's will. Everyone in the world has a cross, but no two crosses are identical. Our Lord's was the Cross of redemption for the sins of the world; Our Lady's was lifelong union with that Cross; and the thief's was the patience on a cross as the prelude to the crown. Our will is the only thing that is absolutely our own; hence it is the perfect offering we can make to God.

— Venerable Fulton J. Sheen

Mother of our Savior, pray for us!

November 22

Believe me: crosses won't be short; the more you improve in the service of God the more suffering will increase. This is God's way, this is the way of all God's servants.

— St. Paul of the Cross

Jesus, crucified for our salvation, have mercy on us!

November 23

And the people stood by, watching; but the rulers scoffed at him, saying, "He saved others; let him save himself, if he is the Christ of God, his Chosen One!" The soldiers also mocked him, coming up and offering him vinegar, and saying, "If you are the King of the Jews, save yourself!" There was also an inscription over him, "This is the King of the Jews."

— LUKE 23:35–38

By Thy anguish and torment, O Lord, deliver us!

November 24

The Lord was no sooner on the Cross than they asked him to come down. "Come down from the Cross" is the most typical demand of an unregenerate world in the face of self-denial and abnegation: a religion without a Cross.

— VENERABLE FULTON J. SHEEN

Lord Jesus, I love Thee.

November 25

Violent force cannot conquer, even though it may triumph for a time. We have the best example of this at the foot of Christ's Cross. Here, too, there was constraint and hatred of the truth. But violence and hatred were conquered by the Lord's love. Let us therefore be powerful in love, by praying for our brothers who have gone astray without condemning anyone, but while unmasking evil. We will go to the resurrection, to victory, through the Cross; there is no other path.

— BLESSED JERZY POPIEŁUSZKO

Jesus, nailed to the Cross, have mercy on us!

November 26

One day our Lord said to Blessed Alan: **"If only these poor wretched sinners would say my Rosary, they would share in the merits of my Passion and I would be their Advocate and would appease my Father's justice."** This life is nothing but warfare and a series of temptations. What better weapon could we use than meditation on the life and Passion of our Lord and Savior Jesus Christ?

— ST. LOUIS DE MONTFORT

By Thy Cross and bitter Passion, O Lord, deliver us!

November 27

If you see that you have not yet suffered tribulations, consider it certain that you have not begun to be a true servant of God; for the Apostle says plainly that all who choose to live piously in Christ, shall suffer persecutions.

— ST. AUGUSTINE OF HIPPO

Lord Jesus Christ, Son of the Living God,
have mercy on me, a sinner.

November 28

The crown of thorns was made of three branches plaited
together, the greatest part of the thorns being purposely
turned inward so as to pierce our Lord's head. Having first
placed these twisted branches on his forehead, they tied them
tightly together at the back of his head, and no sooner was
this accomplished to their satisfaction than they put a large
reed into his hand, and doing all with derisive gravity as if
they were really crowning him king. They seized the reed,
and struck his head so violently that his eyes were filled with
blood; they knelt before him, derided him, spat in his face,
and buffeted him, saying at the same time "Hail, King of the
Jews!' Then they threw down his stool, pulled him up again
from the ground on which he had fallen, and reseated him
with the greatest possible brutality.

— BLESSED ANNE CATHERINE EMMERICH

Jesus, God of peace, have mercy on us!

November 29

Have this mind among yourselves, which was in Christ Jesus, who though he was in the form of God, did not count equality with God a thing to be grasped, but emptied himself, taking the form of a servant, being born in the likeness of men. And being found in human form he humbled himself and became obedient unto death, even death on a cross. Therefore God has highly exalted him and bestowed on him the name which is above every name, that at the name of Jesus every knee should bow, in heaven and on earth and under earth, and every tongue confess that Jesus Christ is Lord, to the glory of God the Father.

— PHILIPPIANS 2:5–11

God, the Father of Heaven, have mercy on us!

November 30

Humility, obedience, meekness, and love are the virtues that shine through the Cross and the Blessed Sacrament of the Altar.

— ST. ANTHONY MARY CLARET

Humility of Jesus, make us humble!

DECEMBER

December 1

Pray that I am of sufficient faith! Like the only model, even following him to the Cross! Pray to Jesus that I may die to all that is not he and his will. Obedience is the last, the highest, and the most perfect of the levels of love. The one at which the self ceases to exist, is abolished, and we die like Jesus on the Cross.

— St. Charles de Foucauld

Christ Jesus, dwell with us and keep us from all harm!

December 2

Nowhere can a man more clearly grasp his dignity than in the mirror of the Cross.

— St. Anthony of Padua

Sure rule of life, save us, O holy Cross!

December 3

O Lord, do not take it [a cross] away from me, unless
to give me a greater.
— ST. FRANCIS XAVIER

O Jesus, grant that others may increase and I may decrease!

December 4

"Where are you from?" But Jesus gave no answer. Pilate
therefore said to him, "You will not speak to me? Do you not
know that I have the power to release you, and the power
to crucify you?" Jesus answered him, **"You would have no
power over me unless it had been given you from above;
therefore he who delivered me to you has the greater sin."**
— JOHN 19:9–11

Precious Blood of Jesus, our strength and power, set us free!

December 5

At three o'clock, implore My mercy, especially for sinners; and, if only for a brief moment, immerse yourself in My Passion, particularly in My abandonment at the moment of agony. This is the hour of great mercy for the whole world. I will allow you to enter into My mortal sorrow. In this hour, I will refuse nothing to the soul that makes a request of Me in virtue of My Passion.

— JESUS TO ST. FAUSTINA KOWALSKA

Jesus, through You we have victory over sin and death!

December 6

By invoking the name of Jesus Christ, who was crucified under Pontius Pilate, Satan is driven out of men.

— ST. IRENAEUS

Jesus, Hope of Christians, save us!

December 7

Although Christ has suffered for all, he has especially suffered for us [priests]. But he that receives more, owes more. Let us render love to him for the blood that he has shed for us.

— ST. AMBROSE

Jesus, light of confessors, have mercy on us!

December 8

All our hope do we repose in the most Blessed Virgin — in the all fair and immaculate one who has crushed the poisonous head of the most cruel serpent and brought salvation to the world: in her who is the glory of the prophets and apostles, the honor of the martyrs, the crown and joy of all the saints.

— BLESSED POPE PIUS IX

Blessed be her holy and Immaculate Conception!

December 9

We glimpse the beauty that is laid up for us when we gaze upon the spiritual beauty your immortal will now creates within our mortal selves. Savior, your crucifixion marked the end of your mortal life; teach us to crucify ourselves and make way for our life in the Spirit.

— St. Ephrem

From all evil, Good Lord, deliver us!

December 10

When Herod saw Jesus, he was very glad, for he had long desired to see him, because he had heard about him, and he was hoping to see some sign done by him. So he questioned him at some length; but he made no answer. The chief priests and the scribes stood by, vehemently accusing him. And Herod with his soldiers treated him with contempt and mocked him; then, clothing him in gorgeous apparel, he sent him back to Pilate. And Herod and Pilate became friends with each other that very day, for before this they had been at enmity with each other.

— Luke 23:8–12

Jesus, condemned to death by Pilate, have mercy on us!

December 11

In the different torments of his sacred body, he gives you the example of heroic penance. Meditate well on the following circumstances: (1) Who is he that suffers? A God holy by essence (2) What does he suffer? Everything that is possible for man to suffer (3) From whom does he suffer it? From those whom he has loaded with benefits (4) Why does he suffer? For your sins (5) How does he suffer? With infinite love. These, in a few words, are the motives and practice of penance.

— St. Ignatius Loyola

Precious Blood of Jesus, save us!

December 12

Great was the sorrow, most bitter grief, of my most holy Son, that not all should make use of the fruits of his Redemption. This same thought also pierced my heart and immensely added to the sorrow of seeing him spit upon, buffeted, and blasphemed more cruelly than can ever be understood by living man.

— Mary to Venerable Mary of Ágreda

Precious Blood of Jesus, Foundation of the world, save us!

December 13

Is it possible to offer, or even imagine, a purer kind of prayer than that which shows mercy to one's torturers by making intercession for them? It was thanks to this kind of prayer that the frenzied persecutors who shed the blood of our Redeemer drank it afterward in faith and proclaimed him to be the Son of God.

— ST. GREGORY THE GREAT

The Lion of the tribe of Judah, the root of David, has conquered!

December 14

The way of suffering is safer, and also more profitable, than that of rejoicing and of action. In suffering, God gives strength, but in action and in joy the soul does but show its own weakness and imperfections.

— ST. JOHN OF THE CROSS

Holy Trinity, One God, have mercy on us!

December 15

Saint Augustine says quite emphatically that there is no spiritual exercise more fruitful or more useful to our salvation than continually turning our thoughts to the sufferings of our Savior. Blessed Albert the Great who had St. Thomas Aquinas as his disciple learned by revelation that by simply thinking of or meditating on the Passion of our Lord Jesus Christ, a Christian gains more merit than if he had fasted on bread and water every Friday for a whole year.

— St. Louis de Montfort

By Thy cries from the Cross, deliver us, Jesus!

December 16

When Christ was crucified, the sun hid its light; when he died, the earth shook in grief. In that earthquake, the rocks were rent, graves were opened, and many bodies of the saints that had been asleep rose and came out of the tombs and appeared to many in the Holy City. If the earth gave signs of recognition when God was delivering his people from the slavery in Egypt by the parting of the waters of the sea, with how much greater reason now did it manifest recognition as the Lord liberated man from the slavery of sin. Though the hearts of the people could not be rent, the rocks could.

— VENERABLE FULTON J. SHEEN

By Thy bloody sweat in the Garden of Gethsemane,
O Lord, deliver us!

December 17

Now the chief priests and the whole council sought testimony against Jesus to put him to death; but they found none. For many bore false witness against him, and their witness did not agree. And some stood up and bore false witness against him, saying "We heard him say, 'I will destroy this temple that is made with hands, and in three days I will build another, not made with hands.'" Yet not even so did their testimony agree.

— MARK 14:55–59

From any denial of Thee, Good Jesus, deliver us!

December 18

They took the body down from the Cross and one of the
few rich men among the first Christians obtained permission
to bury it in a rock tomb in his garden; the Romans setting
a military guard lest there should be some riot and attempt
to recover the body. The whole of that great and glorious
humanity which we call antiquity was gathered up and covered
over; and in that place it was buried. It was the end of a very
great thing called human history; the history that was merely
human. The mythologies and the philosophies were buried
there, the gods and the heroes and the sages. In the great
Roman phrase, they had lived. But as they could only live,
so they could only die; and they were dead.

— G.K. CHESTERTON

Jesus, help me to strip myself of all things that displease Thee!

December 19

Stay willingly on the Cross with Jesus. Drink gladly the
Savior's chalice. Oh! Dear sufferings! Oh! Dear Cross!
Be welcomed!

— ST. PAUL OF THE CROSS

Heart of Jesus, source of life and holiness, heal us!

December 20

When Adam slept, Eve was taken from his side and was called the mother of all living. Now as the second Adam inclined his head and slept on the Cross under the figure of blood and water there came from his side his bride, the Church.

— VENERABLE FULTON J. SHEEN

O Blood and Water, gushing from the side of Jesus, deliver us!

December 21

Take a look now at Calvary. Jesus has died and there is yet no sign of his glorious triumph. It is a good time to examine how much we really want to live as Christians, to be holy. Here is our chance to react against our weaknesses with an act of faith. We can trust in God and resolve to put love into the things we do each day. The experience of sin should lead us to sorrow.

— ST. JOSEMARÍA ESCRIVÁ

Precious Blood of Jesus, Divine Wisdom, save us!

December 22

In the crosses of life that come to us, Jesus offers us opportunities to help him redeem the world. Let us profit by his generosity.

— BLESSED SOLANUS CASEY

Jesus, consolation of the poor, save us!

December 23

He was thinking of me all the time he dragged himself along, up the hill of Calvary. He saw that I should fall again in spite of all former warnings and former assistance. He saw that I should become secure and self-confident, and that my enemy would assail me with some new temptation, to which I never thought I should be exposed.

— ST. JOHN HENRY NEWMAN

In union with the Blessed Virgin Mary and St. Joseph, I love Thee, my God!

December 24

How marvelous the power of the Cross; how great beyond all telling the glory of the Passion: here is the judgment seat of the Lord, the condemnation of the world, the supremacy of Christ crucified.

— St. Leo the Great

Jesus, bearing our sins in Thine own Body on the tree, have mercy on us!

December 25

Though his Body, already exhausted, cried out for water, he would not drink that which would dull his role as mediator. At his birth, his mother was given the gift of myrrh and accepted it as a sign of his ransoming death. At his death, he would refuse the myrrh which would deaden the reason of his coming.

— Venerable Fulton J. Sheen

Jesus, Son of the Blessed Virgin and St. Joseph, have mercy on us!

December 26

You stiff-necked people, uncircumcised in the heart and ears, you always resist the Holy Spirit. As your fathers did, so do you. Which of the prophets did not your fathers persecute? And they killed those who announced beforehand the coming of the Righteous One, whom you have now betrayed and murdered, you who received the law as delivered by angels and did not keep it.

— St. Stephen (Acts of the Apostles 7:51–53)

Saint Stephen, Deacon and Martyr, pray for us!

December 27

When they came to Jesus and saw that he was already dead, they did not break his legs. But one of the soldiers pierced his side with a spear, and at once there came out blood and water. He who saw it has borne witness — his testimony is true, and he knows that he tells the truth — that you may also believe.

— John 19:33–35

Saint John, Apostle and Evangelist, pray for us!

December 28

You please me most when you meditate on My sorrowful Passion. Join your little sufferings to My sorrowful Passion, so that they may have infinite value before My majesty.

— JESUS TO ST. FAUSTINA KOWALSKA

Passion of Christ, strengthen me!

December 29

When day was fading into evening, the Lord laid down his life on the cross, to take it up again; he did not lose his life against his will. The evening sacrifice is then the Passion of the Lord, the Cross of the Lord, the oblation of the victim that brings salvation, the holocaust acceptable to God.

— ST. AUGUSTINE OF HIPPO

By the anguish of Thy Heart upon the Cross, Good Jesus, deliver us!

December 30

Undoubtedly, God in his essence remains above the horizon of human-divine suffering. But Christ's Passion and death pervade, redeem, and ennoble all human suffering, because through the Incarnation he desired to express his solidarity with humanity, which gradually opens to communion with him in faith and love.

— POPE ST. JOHN PAUL II

O holy Cross, wisdom of God, save us!

December 31

A soul that loves God is always ready to please, with every thought, word and action, throughout one's entire existence. And should any affection be sacrificed in order to give joy to God, we should consider ourselves fortunate to have the opportunity to prove our unselfish love. That is why the saints were always willing to make sacrifices and to suffer. In fact, that was how they could prove the purity of their love; in the Cross their love was purified and every affection that was contrary to it was rooted out.

— ST. MAXIMILIAN KOLBE

O holy Cross, vessel of mercy, save us!

REFERENCES

Cover Image: Courtesy of Adobe Stock.

Front quote: St. Paul of the Cross, as quoted in *The Liturgy of the Hours. Volume IV* (New York: Catholic Publishing Co., 1975), 1505.

January Image: Solario Andrea (1473-74–1520). "Christ Carrying the Cross". Public Domain.

January 1: Pope St. John Paul II, *Dives in Misericordia*, 9.

January 2: St. Alphonsus Ligouri, *The Sermons of St. Alphonsus Liguori* (Charlotte, NC: TAN, 1982), 346.

January 3: St. Paul of the Cross, *The Liturgy of the Hours*, Vol. IV (New York: Catholic Book Publishing Co., 1976), 1506.

January 4: 1 John 8–10, *Divine Mercy Catholic Bible, Revised Standard Version, Second Catholic Edition* (West Chester, PA: Ascension Publishing, 2001), 1577.

January 5: St. Maximilian Kolbe, as quoted in *Will to Love, Reflections for Daily Living by St. Maximilian Kolbe, "Prophet of the Civilization of Love,"* trans. Fr. Regis N. Barwig (Libertyville, IL: Marytown Press, 1998), 21.

January 6: Psalms 22: 1–2, 16–18, *Divine Mercy Catholic Bible, Revised Standard Version, Second Catholic Edition* (West Chester, PA: Ascension Publishing, 2001), 708–709.

January 7: St. Basil, *The Liturgy of the Hours*, Vol. II (New York: Catholic Book Publishing Co., 1976), 441.

January 8: *Catechism of the Catholic Church*, par. 571.

January 9: St. Augustine, *The Liturgy of the Hours*, Vol. II (New York: Catholic Book Publishing Co., 1976), 432–433.

January 10: Matthew 26: 38–39, *Divine Mercy Catholic Bible, Revised Standard Version, Second Catholic Edition* (West Chester, PA: Ascension Publishing, 2001), 1307.

January 11: St. John Henry Cardinal Newman, *Prayers Before the Eucharist* (Charlotte, NC: TAN Books, 2019), 30.

January 12: St. Ignatius of Loyola, *The Spiritual Exercises of Saint Ignatius* (Charlotte, NC: TAN Books, 1999), 160.

January 13: St. Teresa of Calcutta, as quoted in Angelo D. Scolozzi, *Jesus, The Word to Be Spoken* (Ann Arbor, MI: Servant Publications, 1998), 115.

January 14: Servant of God Luis Martinez, *Only Jesus,* trans. by Sr. Mary St. Daniel, BVM (London: B. Herder Book Co., 1962), 50.

January 15: St. Anthony Mary Claret, *Autobiography* (Chicago, IL: Claretian Publications, 1976), 138.

January 16: Bl. William Joseph Chaminade, *The Chaminade Legacy: Monograph Series, Document No. 53. Volume 2, 2008,* trans. by Joseph Stefanelli, SM (Dayton, OH: North American Center for Marianist Studies, 2008), 219.

January 17: Hebrews 2: 9–10, *Divine Mercy Catholic Bible, Revised Standard Version, Second Catholic Edition* (West Chester, PA: Ascension Publishing, 2001), 1419.

January 18: St. Gregory Nazianzen, *The Liturgy of the Hours,* Vol. II (New York: Catholic Book Publishing Co., 1976), 393.

January 19: Ven. Sister Maria Vittoria Angelini, as quoted in *Cultivating the Virtues, Self-Mastery With The Saints* (Charlotte, NC: TAN Books, 2016), 136.

January 20: St. Stanislaus Papczyński, *Selected Writings,* trans. by Casimir Krzyzanowski, MIC, Patrick Lynch, MIC, Thaddaeus Lancton, MIC, and J.R. Thomas Holland (Stockbridge, MA: Marian Heritage, 2022), 798.

January 21: St. Maximus the Confessor, *The Liturgy of the Hours Vol. II* (New York: Catholic Book Publishing Co., 1976), 304.

January 22: St. Faustina Kowalska, *Diary: Divine Mercy in My Soul* (Stockbridge, MA: Marian Press, 2005), no. 186–187.

January 23: Thomas à Kempis, *The Imitation of Christ* (San Francisco, CA: Ignatius Press, 2005), bk. 2, no. 12, 98.

January 24: St. Francis De Sales, *Introduction to the Devout Life* (DeKalb, IL: Lighthouse Catholic Media, 2015), part 5, ch. 13, 200.

January 25: St. Paul, 1 Corinthians 1: 18, 22–25, *Divine Mercy Catholic Bible, Revised Standard Version, Second Catholic Edition* (West Chester, PA: Ascension Publishing, 2001), 1479–1480.

January 26: St. John Vianney, The *Sermons of the Cure D'Ars*, trans. by Una Morrissy (Charlotte, NC: TAN Books, 1995), 139.

January 27: Bl. George Matulaitis, *Journal,* trans. by Sister Ann Mikaila, MVS (Lithuania: Marian Fathers), 306.

January 28: St. Thomas Aquinas, *Summa Theologica* (Claremont, CA: Coyote Canyon Press, 2018), Question 69, First Article [III, Q. 69, Art.1] p. 1045.

January 29: St. Faustina Kowalska, *Diary: Divine Mercy in My Soul* (Stockbridge, MA: Marian Press, 2005), no. 1598.

January 30: John 19: 1–3, *Divine Mercy Catholic Bible, Revised Standard Version, Second Catholic Edition* (West Chester, PA: Ascension Publishing, 2001), 1417.

January 31: St. John Bosco, as quoted in Fr. Stefano M. Manelli, FI, *Jesus Our Eucharistic Love* (New Bedford, MA: Academy of the Immaculate, 2017), 27.

February Image: Caravaggio (1571–1610). "Christ Crowned with Thorns". Public Domain.

February 1: Bl. Solanus Casey, as quoted in Br. Leo Wollenweber, O.F.M. Cap., *Meet Solanus Casey* by Brother Leo Wollenweber, O.F.M. Cap. (Cincinnati, OH: St. Anthony Messenger Press, 2002), 125.

February 2: St. Luke 22: 42–44, *Divine Mercy Catholic Bible, Revised Standard Version, Second Catholic Edition* (West Chester, PA: Ascension Publishing, 2001), 1381–1382.

February 3: St. Claude De La Colombière, *The Spiritual Direction of Saint Claude De La Colombière,* trans. by Mother M. Philip, I.B.V.M (San Francisco, CA: Ignatius Press, 2018), 35.

February 4: St. John Vianney, The *Sermons of the Cure D'Ars,* trans. by Una Morrissy (Charlotte, NC: TAN Books, 1995), 180–181.

February 5: St. Methodius of Sicily, *The Liturgy of the Hours,* Vol. II (New York: Catholic Book Publishing Co., 1976), 1662.

February 6: St. Francis De Sales, *The Sign of the Cross* (Manchester, NH: Sophia Institute Press, 2013), 8.

February 7: St. Faustina Kowalska, *Diary: Divine Mercy in My Soul* (Stockbridge, MA: Marian Press, 2005), no. 267.

February 8: St. Maximilian Kolbe, as quoted in *Will to Love, Reflections for Daily Living by St. Maximilian Kolbe, "Prophet of the Civilization of Love,"* trans. Fr. Regis N Barwig (Libertyville, IL: Marytown Press, 1998), 11.

February 9: Bl. Anne Catherine Emmerich, *The Dolorous Passion of Our Lord Jesus Christ* (Charlotte, NC: TAN Books, 2004), 219.

February 10: St. Mother Teresa of Calcutta, *No Greater Love* (Novato, CA: New World Library, 1997), 136.

February 11: St. Claude De La Colombière, *The Spiritual Direction of Saint Claude De La Colombière,* trans. by Mother M. Philip, I.B.V.M (San Francisco, CA: Ignatius Press, 2018), 44.

February 12: St. Louis De Montfort, *The Secret of the Rosary,* trans. by Mary Barbour, T.O.P. (Charlotte, NC: TAN Books, 2013), 65–66.

February 13: Psalm 22: 6–8, *Divine Mercy Catholic Bible, Revised Standard Version, Second Catholic Edition* (West Chester, PA: Ascension Publishing, 2001), 709.

February 14: St. Faustina Kowalska, *Diary: Divine Mercy in My Soul* (Stockbridge, MA: Marian Press, 2005), no. 282.

February 15: Bl. Michael Sopoćko, *The Mercy of God in His Works,* trans. by B. Batchelor (Stockbridge, MA: Marian Fathers, 1962), 225.

February 16: St. Paul of the Cross, *The Liturgy of the Hours,* Vol. IV (New York: Catholic Bok Publishing Co., 1976), 1505.

February 17: *Catechism of the Catholic Church,* par. 1084.

February 18: Ven. Fulton J. Sheen, *Life of Christ* (New York: Image Books, 2008), 421.

February 19: St. Padre Pio, as quoted in *Padre Pio's Words of Hope,* Edited by Eileen Dunn Bertanzetti (Huntington, IN: Our Sunday Visitor, 1999), 39.

February 20: St. Jacinta Marto, as quoted in *Fatima in Lucia's Own Words* (Cambridge, MA: Ravengate Press, 1976), 23.

February 21: St. Paul of the Cross, *A Thought For Every Day, On the Occasion of the 150th Anniversary of the Canonization of St. Paul of the Cross* (Rome, Italy: Convento dei PP Passionisti, 2017), 14.

February 22: St. John the Baptist, as quoted in John 1:36, *Divine Mercy Catholic Bible, Revised Standard Version, Second Catholic Edition* (West Chester, PA: Ascension Publishing, 2001), 1389.

February 23: Pope St. John XXIII, *Journey of a Soul, the Autobiography of Pope John XXIII* (New York: Image Books, 1980), 369.

February 24: Revelation 12: 10–12, *Divine Mercy Catholic Bible, Revised Standard Version, Second Catholic Edition* (West Chester, PA: Ascension Publishing, 2001), 1594.

February 25: St. Thomas Aquinas, *Summa Theologica*, Question 73, Fifth Article [III, Q. 73, Art.5] p. 1058 (Claremont, CA: Coyote Canyon Press, 2018).

February 26: Ven. Fulton J. Sheen, *Life of Christ* (New York: Doubleday, 1977), 319–320.

February 27: St. John Vianney, The *Sermons of the Cure D'Ars*, trans. by Una Morrissy (Charlotte, NC: TAN Books, 1995), 182.

February 28: St. Faustina Kowalska, *Diary: Divine Mercy in My Soul* (Stockbridge, MA: Marian Press, 2005), no. 369.

February 29: St. Maximilian Kolbe, as quoted in *Will to Love, Reflections for Daily Living by St. Maximilian Kolbe, "Prophet of the Civilization of Love,"* trans. Fr. Regis N Barwig (Libertyville, IL: Marytown Press, 1998), 16.

March Image: Matthias Stom (1615–1649). "Christ Crowned with Thorns". Public Domain.

March 1: St. Faustina Kowalska, *Diary: Divine Mercy in My Soul* (Stockbridge, MA: Marian Press, 2005), no. 965.

March 2: Ven. Fulton J. Sheen, *Life of Christ* (New York: Doubleday, 1977), 345.

March 3: Lamentations 1:12, *Divine Mercy Catholic Bible, Revised Standard Version, Second Catholic Edition* (West Chester, PA: Ascension Publishing, 2001), 1069.

March 4: Thomas à Kempis, *The Imitation of Christ*, trans. by Ronald Knox (San Francisco, CA: Ignatius Press, 2005), bk. 2, no. 12, 99.

March 5: Servant of God Ida Peterfy, *With Christ to Calvary*. Society Devoted to the Sacred Heart (2020), page 11. Available as a PDF at www.sacredheartsisters. com.

March 6: Bl. George Kaszyra, "Spiritual Conference," (*Conciones,* January 22, 1931). Collegium Romanum, No. 12. General Archives, Marian Fathers (Rome).

March 7: St. Augustine of Hippo, as quoted in *Cultivating the Virtues, Self-Mastery With The Saints* (Charlotte, NC: TAN Books, 2016), 143.

March 8: Matthew 17: 22–23, *Divine Mercy Catholic Bible, Revised Standard Version, Second Catholic Edition* (West Chester, PA: Ascension Publishing, 2001), 1292.

March 9: Pope Benedict XVI, *Behold The Pierced One* (San Francisco, CA: Ignatius Press, 1986), 109.

March 10: St. John Vianney, as quoted in Fr. Stefano M. Manelli, FI. *Jesus Our Eucharistic Love* (New Bedford, MA: Academy of the Immaculate, 2017), 98.

March 11: Bl. Dina Bélanger, *Autobiography* (Montreal: Les Religieuses de Jesus-Marie, 1997), 222.

March 12: St. Luke 23: 46–48, *Divine Mercy Catholic Bible, Revised Standard Version, Second Catholic Edition* (West Chester, PA: Ascension Publishing, 2001), 1384.

March 13: St. Ignatius of Antioch, as quoted in St. Francis de Sales, *The Sign of the Cross* (Manchester, NH: Sophia Institute Press, 2013), 79–80.

March 14: St. Faustina Kowalska, *Diary: Divine Mercy in My Soul* (Stockbridge, MA: Marian Press, 2005), no. 408.

March 15: Ven. Fulton J. Sheen, *Life of Christ* (New York: Image Books, 2008), 459.

March 16: St. Paul of the Cross, *A Though For Every Day, On the Occasion of the 150ᵗʰ Anniversary of the Canonization of St. Paul of the Cross* (Rome: Convento dei PP Passionisti, 2017), 14.

March 17: St. Patrick, as quoted in *Manual for Spiritual Warfare: The Breastplate of St. Patrick* (Charlotte, NC: TAN Books, 2014), 255–256.

March 18: St. Anthony Mary Claret, *Autobiography* (Chicago, IL: Claretian Publications, 1976), 140.

March 19: St. John Henry Newman, *Prayers Before the Eucharist* (Charlotte, NC: TAN Books, 2019), 16.

March 20: St. Francis De Sales, *Introduction to the Devout Life* (DeKalb, IL: Lighthouse Catholic Media, 2015), part 5, ch. 13, 200.

March 21: Ven. Mary of Ágreda, *The Mystical City of God*. Vol. III, trans. Rev. George J. Blatter (Charlotte, NC: TAN Books, 2006), no. 591.

March 22: St. Andrew of Crete, *The Liturgy of the Hours*, Vol. II (New York: Catholic Book Publishing Co., 1976), 419.

March 23: St. Mother Teresa of Calcutta, as quoted in *No Greater Love*, Edited by Becky Benenate and Joseph Durepos (Novato, CA: New World Library, 1997), 137.

March 24: St. Alphonsus Ligouri, *The Sermons of St. Alphonsus Liguori* (Charlotte, NC: TAN Books, 1982), 348.

March 25: Bl. Maria Concepción Cabrera de Armida, *Roses and Thorns*, edited by Ron Leonardo (Staten Island, NY: Society of St. Paul, 2007), 108.

March 26: St. Padre Pio, as quoted in *Padre Pio's Words of Hope*, Edited by Eileen Dunn Bertanzetti (Huntington, IN: Our Sunday Visitor, 1999), 39.

March 27: St. Maximilian Kolbe, as quoted in *Will to Love, Reflections for Daily Living by St. Maximilian Kolbe, "Prophet of the Civilization of Love,"* trans. Fr. Regis N Barwig (Libertyville, IL: Marytown Press, 1998), 22–23.

March 28: Mark 14: 43–46, *Divine Mercy Catholic Bible, Revised Standard Version, Second Catholic Edition* (West Chester, PA: Ascension Publishing, 2001), 1335.

March 29: Servant of God Luis Martinez, *Only Jesus,* trans. by Sr. Mary St. Daniel, BVM (London: B. Herder Book Co., 1962), 79.

March 30: St. John Henry Newman, *Prayers Before the Eucharist* (Charlotte, NC: TAN Books, 2019), 30.

March 31: Pope St. John Paul II, *On the Christian Meaning of Human Suffering* (Boston, MA: Pauline Books & Media, 2014), 69.

April Image: Albrecht Dürer (1471–1528). "Christ Carrying the Cross". Public Domain.

April 1: St. Melito of Sardis, *The Liturgy of the Hours,* Vol. II (New York: Catholic Book Publishing Co., 1976), 459.

April 2: St. Francis of Paola, *The Liturgy of the Hours,* Vol. II (New York: Catholic Book Publishing Co., 1976, 1757–1758.

April 3: St. Clement, *The Liturgy of the Hours,* Vol. II (New York: Catholic Book Publishing Co., 1976), 51.

April 4: St. Fulgentius of Ruspe, *The Liturgy of the Hours,* Vol. II (New York: Catholic Book Publishing Co., 1976), 384.

April 5: St. Vincent Ferrer, as quoted in *Cultivating the Virtues, Self-Mastery With The Saints*, Trans (Charlotte, NC: TAN Books, 2016), 155.

April 6: St. Gregory Nazianzen, *The Liturgy of the Hours,* Vol. II (New York: Catholic Book Publishing Co., 1976), 393.

April 7: St. John Baptist De La Salle, *The Liturgy of the Hours,* Vol. II (New York: Catholic Book Publishing Co., 1976), 1766.

April 8: St. Faustina Kowalska, *Diary: Divine Mercy in My Soul* (Stockbridge, MA: Marian Press, 2005), no. 379.

April 9: John 18:19–23, *Divine Mercy Catholic Bible, Revised Standard Version, Second Catholic Edition* (West Chester, PA: Ascension Publishing, 2001), 1416–1417.

April 10: *The Catechism of the Council of Trent*, trans. by John A. McHugh, O.P. and Charles J Callan, O.P. (Charlotte, NC: TAN Books, 1982), 51.

April 11: Ven. Fulton J. Sheen, *Life of Christ* (New York: Doubleday, 1977), 316.

April 12: St. Ignatius of Loyola, *The Spiritual Exercises of Saint Ignatius* (Charlotte, NC: TAN Books, 1999), 156.

April 13: St. John of the Cross, as quoted in *Cultivating the Virtues, Self-Mastery With The Saints* (Charlotte, NC: TAN Books, 2016), 133–134.

April 14: Ven. Fulton J. Sheen, *Life of Christ* (New York: Image Books, 2008), 487.

April 15: St. Maximilian Kolbe, as quoted in *Will to Love, Reflections for Daily Living by St. Maximilian Kolbe, "Prophet of the Civilization of Love,"* trans. Fr. Regis N Barwig (Libertyville, IL: Marytown Press, 1998), 22.

April 16: St. Bernadette Soubirous, as quoted in Fr. Stefano M. Manelli, FI, *Jesus Our Eucharistic Love* (New Bedford, MA: Academy of the Immaculate, 2017), 26.

April 17: St. Paul of the Cross, *A Though For Every Day, On the Occasion of the 150th Anniversary of the Canonization of St. Paul of the Cross* (Rome: Convento dei PP Passionisti, 2017), 22.

April 18: Isaiah 52:13–15, *Divine Mercy Catholic Bible, Revised Standard Version, Second Catholic Edition* (West Chester, PA: Ascension Publishing, 2001), 981.

April 19: Pope St. John Paul II, *Dives in Misericordia*, 7.

April 20: St. John Henry Newman, *Prayers Before the Eucharist* (Charlotte, NC: TAN Books, 2019), 32.

April 21: St. Anthony Mary Claret, *Autobiography* (Chicago, IL: Claretian Publications, 1976), 139.

April 22: St. Mother Teresa of Calcutta, as quoted in Jose Luis Gonzalez Balado, *Mother Teresa In My Own Words* (Liguori, MO: Liguori Publications, 1997), 81.

April 23: St. Stanislaus Papczyński, *Selected Writings*, trans. by Casimir Krzyzanowski, MIC, Patrick Lynch, MIC, Thaddaeus Lancton, MIC, and J.R. Thomas Holland (Stockbridge, MA: Marian Heritage, 2022), 776.

April 24: St. Francis De Sales, as quoted in *Cultivating the Virtues, Self-Mastery With The Saints* (Charlotte, NC: TAN Books, 2016), 151–152.

April 25: St. Mark 15: 12–15, *Divine Mercy Catholic Bible, Revised Standard Version, Second Catholic Edition* (West Chester, PA: Ascension Publishing, 2001), 1337.

April 26: St. Faustina Kowalska, *Diary: Divine Mercy in My Soul* (Stockbridge, MA: Marian Press, 2005), no. 482.

April 27: Bl. Anne Catherine Emmerich, *The Dolorous Passion of Our Lord Jesus Christ* (Charlotte, NC: TAN Books, 2004), 166.

April 28: St. Louis De Montfort, *The Secret of the Rosary*, trans. Mary Barbour, T.O.P. (Bay Shore, NY: Montfort Publications, 2013), 66.

April 29: St. Catherine of Siena, *The Dialogue*, trans. by Algar Thorold (Australia: Cana Press, 2021), 93.

April 30: St. Padre Pio, as quoted in Gianluigi Pasquale, *Padre Pio's Spiritual Direction For Every Day,* trans. by Marsha Daigle-Williamson (Cincinnati, OH: Servant, 2011), 38.

May Image: North Netherlandish (Bruges) Painer (ca. 1470). "Christ Bearing the Cross". Public Domain.

May 1: St. Mary Magdalen de Pazzi, as quoted in Fr. Anthony-Joseph Patrignani, SJ, *A Manual of Practical Devotion to St. Joseph* (Charlotte, NC: TAN Books, 2012), 179.

May 2: John 18: 36–38, *Divine Mercy Catholic Bible, Revised Standard Version, Second Catholic Edition* (West Chester, PA: Ascension Publishing, 2001), 1417.

May 3: St. Padre Pio, as quoted in Gianluigi Pasquale, *Padre Pio's Spiritual Direction For Every Day,* trans. by Marsha Daigle-Williamson (Cincinnati, OH: Servant, 2011), 36.

May 4: Mark 15: 21–25, *Divine Mercy Catholic Bible, Revised Standard Version, Second Catholic Edition* (West Chester, PA: Ascension Publishing, 2001), 1337.

May 5: Pope St. John Paul II, as quoted in Fr. Stefano M. Manelli, FI, *Jesus Our Eucharistic Love* (New Bedford, MA: Academy of the Immaculate, 2017), 25.

May 6: St. Ignatius of Loyola, *The Spiritual Exercises of Saint Ignatius* (Charlotte, NC: TAN Books, 1999), 156.

May 7: Bl. James Alberione, *Mary, Hope of the World,* trans. by Hilda Calabro, M.A (Boston, MA: St. Paul Editions, 1981), 146.

May 8: Isaiah 53:3–5, *Divine Mercy Catholic Bible, Revised Standard Version, Second Catholic Edition* (West Chester, PA: Ascension Publishing, 2001), 981–982.

May 9: Bl. Dina Bélanger, *Autobiography* (Montreal: Les Religieuses de Jesus-Marie, 1997), 229.

May 10: St. Francis De Sales, *Roses Among Thorns*, edited and trans. by Christopher O. Blum (Manchester, NH: Sophia Institute Press, 2014), 104.

May 11: G.K. Chesterton, *The Everyman Chesterton*, edited by Ian Ker (London: Everyman's Library, 2011), 439.

May 12: *The Catechism of the Council of Trent*, trans. By John A. McHugh, O.P. and Charles J Callan, O.P. (Charlotte, NC: TAN Books, 1982), 51–52.

May 13: John 19: 26–27, *Divine Mercy Catholic Bible, Revised Standard Version, Second Catholic Edition* (West Chester, PA: Ascension Publishing, 2001), 1419.

May 14: Bl. Michael Sopoćko, *The Mercy of God in His Works*, trans. by B. Batchelor (Stockbridge, MA: Marian Fathers, 1962), 226–227.

May 15: Pope St. John Paul II, *Dives in Misericordia*, 8.

May 16: St. Faustina Kowalska, *Diary: Divine Mercy in My Soul* (Stockbridge, MA: Marian Press, 2005), no. 737–738.

May 17: Bl. Anne Catherine Emmerich, *The Dolorous Passion of Our Lord Jesus Christ* (Charlotte, NC: TAN Books, 2004), 257.

May 18: St. Stanislaus Papczyński, *Selected Writings*, trans. by Casimir Krzyzanowski, MIC, Patrick Lynch, MIC, Thaddaeus Lancton, MIC, and J.R. Thomas Holland (Stockbridge, MA: Marian Heritage, 2022), 761.

May 19: *The Catechism of the Council of Trent*, trans. by John A. McHugh, O.P. and Charles J Callan, O.P. (Charlotte, NC: TAN Books, 1982), 52.

May 20: Bl. Basil Moreau, *Basil Moreau Essential Writings*, edited by Kevin Grove, CSC and Andrew Gawrych, CSC (Notre Dame, IN: Christian Classics, 2014), 283.

May 21: St. Paul, Romans 3: 23–25, *Divine Mercy Catholic Bible, Revised Standard Version, Second Catholic Edition* (West Chester, PA: Ascension Publishing, 2001), 1462–1463.

May 22: St. Paul of the Cross, *A Though For Every Day, On the Occasion of the 150th Anniversary of the Canonization of St. Paul of the Cross* (Rome: Convento dei PP Passionisti, 2017), 44.

May 23: Pope St. John XXIII, Journey of a Soul, the Autobiography of Pope John XXIII (New York: Image Books, 1980), 370.

May 24: Ven. Mary of Ágreda, *The Mystical City of God*. Vol. III, trans. Rev. George J. Blatter (Charlotte, NC: TAN Books, 2006), 547.

May 25: Pope Benedict XVI, *Behold The Pierced One* (San Francisco, CA: Ignatius Press, 1986), 22.

May 26: St. Philip Neri, as quoted in *Cultivating the Virtues, Self-Mastery With The Saints*, Trans (Charlotte, NC: TAN Books, 2016), 158.

May 27: St. Mother Teresa of Calcutta, as quoted in Jose Luis Gonzalez Balado, *Mother Teresa In My Own Words* (Liguori, MO: Liguori Publications, 1997), 86.

May 28: St. John Vianney, The *Sermons of the Cure D'Ars*, trans. by Una Morrissy (Charlotte, NC: TAN Books, 1995), 176.

May 29: St. Catherine of Siena, as quoted in *Cultivating the Virtues, Self-Mastery With The Saints* (Charlotte, NC: TAN Books, 2016), 146.

May 30: Mark 14: 61–65, *Divine Mercy Catholic Bible, Revised Standard Version, Second Catholic Edition* (West Chester, PA: Ascension Publishing, 2001), 1336.

May 31: St. Louis De Montfort, *True Devotion to the Blessed Virgin* (Bay Shore, NY: Montfort Publications, 1980), 75–76.

June Image: Grégoire Huret (1606–1670). "Christ Carrying the Cross". Public Domain.

June 1: St. Augustine of Hippo, *The Liturgy of the Hours*, Vol. IV (New York: Catholic Book Publishing Co., 1976), 1304.

June 2: Bl. Basil Moreau, *Basil Moreau Essential Writings*, edited by Kevin Grove, CSC and Andrew Gawrych, CSC (Notre Dame, IN: Christian Classics, 2014), 324.

June 3: Matthew 26: 74–75, *Divine Mercy Catholic Bible, Revised Standard Version, Second Catholic Edition* (West Chester, PA: Ascension Publishing, 2001), 1308.

June 4: St. John of the Cross, as quoted in *Cultivating the Virtues, Self-Mastery With The Saints* (Charlotte, NC: TAN Books, 2016), 135.

June 5: St. Bernard of Clairvaux, *The Classics of Western Spirituality, Bernard of Clairvaux, Selected Works*, trans. by G.R. Evans (New York: Paulist Press, 1987), 44.

June 6: St. Francis De Sales, *Introduction to the Devout Life* (San Francisco, CA: Ignatius Press, 1997), 200–201.

June 7: Bl. Solanus Casey, as quoted in *Meet Solanus Casey* by Brother Leo Wollenweber, O.F.M. Cap (Cincinnati, OH: St. Anthony Messenger Press, 2002), 125.

June 8: St. Maximilian Kolbe, as quoted in *Will to Love, Reflections for Daily Living by St. Maximilian Kolbe, "Prophet of the Civilization of Love,"* trans. Fr. Regis N Barwig (Libertyville, IL: Marytown Press, 1998), 104–105.

June 9: Servant of God Luis Martinez, *Only Jesus,* trans. by Sr. Mary St. Daniel, BVM (London: B. Herder Book Co., 1962), 141.

June 10: Bl. Anne Catherine Emmerich, *The Dolorous Passion of Our Lord Jesus Christ* (Charlotte, NC: TAN Books, 2004), 258.

June 11: St. John Vianney, The *Sermons of the Curé D'Ars,* trans. By Una Morrissy (Charlotte, NC: TAN Books, 1995), 174.

June 12: Luke 12: 49–50, *Divine Mercy Catholic Bible, Revised Standard Version, Second Catholic Edition* (West Chester, PA: Ascension Publishing, 2001), 1366.

June 13: St. Anthony of Padua, as quoted in Sophronius Clasen, O.F.M., *Saint Anthony Doctor of the Church* (Chicago, IL: Franciscan Herald Press, 1960), 42.

June 14: *The Catechism of the Council of Trent,* trans. by John A. McHugh, O.P. and Charles J Callan, O.P. (Charlotte, NC: TAN Books, 1982), 53.

June 15: St. Faustina Kowalska, *Diary: Divine Mercy in My Soul* (Stockbridge, MA: Marian Press, 2005), no. 811.

June 16: Isaiah 53:7, *Divine Mercy Catholic Bible, Revised Standard Version, Second Catholic Edition* (West Chester, PA: Ascension Publishing, 2001), 982.

June 17: Thomas à Kempis, *The Imitation of Christ,* trans. by Ronald Knox (San Francisco, CA: Ignatius Press, 2005), 96.

June 18: St. Padre Pio, as quoted in Gianluigi Pasquale, *Padre Pio's Spiritual Direction For Every Day,* trans. by Marsha Daigle-Williamson (Cincinnati, OH: Servant, 2011), 37.

June 19: St. Mother Teresa of Calcutta, as quoted in Jose Luis Gonzalez Balado, *Mother Teresa In My Own Words* (Liguori, MO: Liguori Publications, 1997), 86.

June 20: St. John Vianney, The *Sermons of the Curé D'Ars,* trans. by Una Morrissy (Charlotte, NC: TAN Books, 1995), 177.

June 21: St. Teresa of Ávila, as quoted in *Cultivating the Virtues, Self-Mastery With The Saints* (Charlotte, NC: TAN Books, 2016), 161.

June 22: Pope St. John Paul II, *On the Christian Meaning of Human Suffering,* 52.

June 23: St. Stanislaus Papczyński, *Selected Writings,* trans. by Casimir Krzyzanowski, MIC, Patrick Lynch, MIC, Thaddaeus Lancton, MIC, and J.R. Thomas Holland (Stockbridge, MA: Marian Heritage, 2022), 799.

June 24: St. Augustine of Hippo, *The Liturgy of the Hours,* Vol. III (New York: Catholic Book Publishing Co., 1976), 1488–1489.

REFERENCES

June 25: Bl. Anne Catherine Emmerich, *The Dolorous Passion of Our Lord Jesus Christ* (Charlotte, NC: TAN Books, 2004), 100.

June 26: St. Josemaría Escrivá, *Christ is Passing By* (Rochelle, NY: Little Hills Press, 1990), 136–137.

June 27: Bl. Maria Concepción Cabrera de Armida, *Roses and Thorns*, ed. by Ron Leonardo (Staten Island, NY: Society of St. Paul, 2007), 109.

June 28: St. Paul of the Cross, *A Though For Every Day, On the Occasion of the 150th Anniversary of the Canonization of St. Paul of the Cross* (Rome: Convento dei PP Passionisti, 2017), 5.

June 29: 1 Corinthians 15: 3–8, *Divine Mercy Catholic Bible, Revised Standard Version, Second Catholic Edition* (West Chester, PA: Ascension Publishing, 2001), 1493.

June 30: St. Martial, as quoted in St. Francis De Sales, *The Sign of the Cross* (Manchester, NH: Sophia Institute Press, 2013), 79.

July Image: Domenico Fetti (1589–1623). "The Veil of Veronica". Public Domain.

July 1: St. Francis De Sales, *Roses Among Thorns*, Edited and trans. Christopher O. Blum (Manchester, NH: Sophia Institute Press, 2014), 70.

July 2: Second Vatican Council (Gaudium Et Spes, nn. 37–38).

July 3: St. Anthony of Padua, as quoted in Sophronius Clasen, O.F.M., *Saint Anthony Doctor of the Church* (Chicago, IL: Franciscan Herald Press, 1960), 41.

July 4: St. Andrew of Crete, *The Liturgy of the Hours Vol. IV* (New York: Catholic Book Publishing Co., 1976), 1390.

July 5: Bl. Dina Bélanger, *Autobiography* (Montreal: Les Religieuses de Jesus-Marie, 1997), 230.

July 6: St. John Fisher, *The Liturgy of the Hours*, Vol. II (New York: Catholic Book Publishing Co., 1976), 351.

July 7: Bl. Basil Moreau, *Basil Moreau Essential Writings*, edited by Kevin Grove, CSC and Andrew Gawrych, CSC (Notre Dame, IN: Christian Classics, 2014), 284.

July 8: Luke 23: 28–31, *Divine Mercy Catholic Bible, Revised Standard Version, Second Catholic Edition* (West Chester, PA: Ascension Publishing, 2001), 1383–1384.

July 9: St. Padre Pio, as quoted in Gianluigi Pasquale, *Padre Pio's Spiritual Direction For Every Day,* trans. by Marsha Daigle-Williamson (Cincinnati, OH: Servant, 2011), 33.

July 10: Bl. Maria Concepción Cabrera de Armida, *Roses and Thorns,* edited by Ron Leonardo (Staten Island, NY: Society of St. Paul, 2007), 109.

July 11: Ven. Fulton J. Sheen, *Life of Christ* (New York: Doubleday, 1977), 349.

July 12: St. Faustina Kowalska, *Diary: Divine Mercy in My Soul* (Stockbridge, MA: Marian Press, 2005), no. 378.

July 13: Isaiah 53:12, *Divine Mercy Catholic Bible, Revised Standard Version, Second Catholic Edition* (West Chester, PA: Ascension Publishing, 2001), 982.

July 14: St. Paul of the Cross, *A Though For Every Day, On the Occasion of the 150th Anniversary of the Canonization of St. Paul of the Cross* (Rome: Convento dei PP Passionisti, 2017), 9.

July 15: St. Bonaventure, *The Journey of the Mind to God,* trans. by Philotheus Boehner, O.F.M (Indianapolis, IN: Hackett Publishing Company, 1993), 2.

July 16: Pope St. John Paul II, *Dives in Misericordia,* 7.

July 17: *The Catechism of the Council of Trent,* trans. by John A. McHugh, O.P. and Charles J Callan, O.P. (Charlotte, NC: TAN Books, 1982), 55.

July 18: St. John Henry Newman, *Prayers Before the Eucharist* (Charlotte, NC: TAN Books, 2019, 32.

July 19: St. John Vianney, The *Sermons of the Curé D'Ars,* trans. by Una Morrissy (Charlotte, NC: TAN Books, 1995), 77.

July 20: St. Mother Teresa of Calcutta, as quoted in Jose Luis Gonzalez Balado, *Mother Teresa In My Own Words* (Liguori, MO: Liguori Publications, 1997), 86.

July 21: St. Gregory Nazianzen, *The Liturgy of the Hours,* Vol. II (New York: Catholic Book Publishing Co., 1976), 393.

July 22: St. Louis De Montfort, *The Secret of the Rosary,* trans. Mary Barbour, T.O.P. (Bay Shore, NY: Montfort Publications, 2013), 73–74.

July 23: St. Bridget, *Revelations of St. Bridget On The Life And Passion Of Our Lord And The Life Of His Blessed Mother* (Charlotte, NC: TAN Books, 2015), 44–45.

July 24: St. Mary Magdalene De Pazzi, *The Liturgy of the Hours,* Vol. II (New York: Catholic Book Publishing Co., 1976), 1836–1837.

July 25: St. Vincent Ferrer, *Treatise on The Spiritual Life* (Westminster, MD: The Newman Book Shop, 1946), 50.

REFERENCES

July 26: Ven. Fulton J. Sheen, *Life of Christ* (New York: Image Books, 2008), 493.

July 27: St. Alphonsus De Liguori, *Dignity and Duties of the Priest* (Brooklyn, NY: Redemptorist Fathers, 1927), 387.

July 28: G.K. Chesterton, as quoted by Dale Ahlquist, *C.K. Chesterton, The Apostle of Common Sense* (San Francisco, CA: Ignatius Press, 2003), 122.

July 29: St. Lupus, as quoted in *Cultivating the Virtues, Self-Mastery With The Saints* (Charlotte, NC: TAN Books, 2016), 151–152.

July 30: Bl. Solanus Casey, as quoted in Br. Leo Wollenweber, O.F.M., *Meet Solanus Casey* (Cincinnati, OH: St. Anthony Messenger Press, 2002), 125.

July 31: St. Ignatius of Loyola, *The Spiritual Exercises of Saint Ignatius* (Charlotte, NC: TAN Books, 1999), 157.

August Image: Guercino (1591–1666). "The Flagellation of Christ". Public Domain.

August 1: St. Thomas Aquinas, as quoted in *The Aquinas Prayer Book, The Prayers and Hymns of St. Thomas Aquinas,* edited and trans. by Robert Anderson and Johann Moser (Manchester, NH: Sophia Institute Press, 2000), 69–70.

August 2: Ven. Fulton J. Sheen, *These are the Sacraments* (New York: Image Books, 1964), 26.

August 3: Pope St. John Paul II, *On the Christian Meaning of Human Suffering*, 58.

August 4: St. John Vianney, The *Sermons of the Curé D'Ars*, trans. by Una Morrissy (Charlotte, NC: TAN Books, 1995), 176.

August 5: Bl. William Joseph Chaminade, *Marian Writings. Volume 1,* trans. by Henry Bradley, SM & Joseph H. Roy, SM (Dayton, OH: Marianist Resources Commission, 1980), 214–215.

August 6: St. John Henry Newman, *Prayers Before the Eucharist* (Charlotte, NC: TAN Books, 2019), 58.

August 7: St. Leo the Great, *The Liturgy of the Hours*, Vol. II (New York: Catholic Book Publishing Co., 1976), 359–360.

August 8: St. Padre Pio, as quoted in Gianluigi Pasquale, *Padre Pio's Spiritual Direction For Every Day,* trans. by Marsha Daigle-Williamson (Cincinnati, OH: Servant, 2011), 34.

August 9: Ven. Fulton J. Sheen, *Life of Christ* (New York: Doubleday, 1977), 356.

August 10: St. Augustine of Hippo, *The Liturgy of the Hours*, Vol. IV (New York: Catholic Book Publishing Co., 1976), 1306.

August 11: St. Clare of Assisi, as quoted in Clair Marie Ledoux, *Clare of Assisi, Her Spirituality Revealed in Her Letters* (Cincinnati, OH:, St. Anthony Messenger Press, 2003), 81.

August 12: St. Francis De Sales, as quoted in *Cultivating the Virtues, Self-Mastery With The Saints* (Charlotte, NC: TAN Books, 2016), 147.

August 13: Mark 15: 42–46, *Divine Mercy Catholic Bible, Revised Standard Version, Second Catholic Edition* (West Chester, PA: Ascension Publishing, 2001), 1384.

August 14: St. Maximilian Kolbe, as quoted in *Will to Love, Reflections for Daily Living by St. Maximilian Kolbe, "Prophet of the Civilization of Love,"* trans. Fr. Regis N Barwig (Libertyville, IL: Marytown Press, 1998), 102.

August 15: St. Louis De Montfort, *The Secret of Mary* (Charlotte, NC: TAN Books, 1998), 20.

August 16: St. Mother Teresa of Calcutta, as quoted in Jose Luis Gonzalez Balado, *Mother Teresa In My Own Words* (Liguori, MO: Liguori Publications, 1997), 88.

August 17: Bl. Anne Catherine Emmerich, *The Dolorous Passion of Our Lord Jesus Christ* (Charlotte, NC: TAN Books, 2004), 219.

August 18: St. Faustina Kowalska, *Diary: Divine Mercy in My Soul* (Stockbridge, MA: Marian Press, 2005), no. 1016.

August 19: *The Catechism of the Council of Trent*, trans. by John A. McHugh, O.P. and Charles J Callan, O.P. (Charlotte, NC: TAN Books, 1982), 58.

August 20: St. Bernard of Clairvaux, as quoted in St. Louis de Montfort, *The Secret of the Rosary*, trans. Mary Barbour, T.O.P. (Bay Shore, NY: Montfort Publications, 2013), 67.

August 21: Pope St. Pius X, *Ad Diem Illum Laetissimum*, 12.

August 22: St. Faustina Kowalska, *Diary: Divine Mercy in My Soul* (Stockbridge, MA: Marian Press, 2005), no. 1032.

August 23: Luke 24: 18–21, *Divine Mercy Catholic Bible, Revised Standard Version, Second Catholic Edition* (West Chester, PA: Ascension Publishing, 2001), 1385.

August 24: St. Stanislaus Papczyński, *Selected Writings*, trans. by Casimir Krzyzanowski, MIC, Patrick Lynch, MIC, Thaddaeus Lancton, MIC, and J.R. Thomas Holland (Stockbridge, MA: Marian Heritage, 2022), 791.

REFERENCES

August 25: St. Paul of the Cross, *A Though For Every Day, On the Occasion of the 150ᵗʰ Anniversary of the Canonization of St. Paul of the Cross* (Rome: Convento dei PP Passionisti, 2017), 8.

August 26: St. Claude De La Colombière, *The Spiritual Direction of Saint Claude De La Colombière,* trans. by Mother M. Philip, I.B.V.M (San Francisco, CA: Ignatius Press, 2018), 82.

August 27: St. Thérèse of Lisieux, *The Story of a Soul,* trans. by John Beevers (New York: Image Books, 2001), 53.

August 28: St. Augustine, *The Liturgy of the Hours,* Vol. II (New York: Catholic Book Publishing Co., 1976), 432–433.

August 29: St. Bede the Venerable, *The Liturgy of the Hours*, Vol. IV (New York: Catholic Book Publishing Co., 1976), 1359.

August 30: Ven. Fulton J. Sheen, *Life of Christ* (New York: Doubleday, 1977), 370.

August 31: Servant of God Luis Martinez, *Only Jesus,* trans. by Sr. Mary St. Daniel, BVM (London: B. Herder Book Co., 1962), 84.

September Image: Abraham Janssens van Nuyssen (1575–1632). "Calvary". Public Domain.

September 1: Matthew 27: 20–23, *Divine Mercy Catholic Bible, Revised Standard Version, Second Catholic Edition* (West Chester, PA: Ascension Publishing, 2001), 1308–1309.

September 2: Ven. Fulton J. Sheen, *Life of Christ* (New York: Image Books, 2008), 507.

September 3: St. Gregory the Great, *The Liturgy of the Hours*, Vol. II (New York: Catholic Book Publishing Co., 1976), 257–258.

September 4: Bl. Dina Bélanger, *Autobiography* (Montreal: Les Religieuses de Jesus-Marie, 1997), 290.

September 5: St. Teresa of Calcutta, *The Joy In Loving, Mother Teresa* (New York, NY: Penguin Compass, 2000), 125.

September 6: St. John Fisher, *The Liturgy of the Hours*, Vol. II (New York: Catholic Book Publishing Co., 1976), 351.

September 7: St. Faustina Kowalska, *Diary: Divine Mercy in My Soul* (Stockbridge, MA: Marian Press, 2005), no. 1184 & no. 1657.

September 8: Bl. Anne Catherine Emmerich, *The Dolorous Passion of Our Lord Jesus Christ* (Charlotte, NC: TAN Books, 2004), 172.

September 9: St. Ambrose, as quoted in St. Francis de Sales, *The Sign of the Cross* (Manchester, NH: Sophia Institute Press, 2013), 18.

September 10: Bl. Michael Sopoćko, *The Mercy of God in His Works*, trans. by B. Batchelor (Stockbridge, MA: Marian Fathers, 1962), 202.

September 11: *The Catechism of the Council of Trent*, trans. by John A. McHugh, O.P. and Charles J Callan, O.P. (Charlotte, NC: TAN Books, 1982), 60.

September 12: St. Louis De Montfort, *The Secret of the Rosary*. trans. Mary Barbour, T.O.P. (Bay Shore, NY: Montfort Publications, 2013), 68.

September 13: St. John Chrysostom, as quoted in *Cultivating the Virtues, Self-Mastery With The Saints* (Charlotte, NC: TAN Books, 2016), 138.

September 14: St. Andrew of Crete, *The Liturgy of the Hours Vol. IV* (New York: Catholic Book Publishing Co., 1976), 1390.

September 15: Bl. Basil Moreau, *Basil Moreau Essential Writings*, edited by Kevin Grove, CSC and Andrew Gawrych, CSC (Notre Dame, IN: Christian Classics, 2014), 290.

September 16: St. Cyprian as quoted in St. Francis de Sales, *The Sign of the Cross* (Manchester, NH: Sophia Institute Press, 2013), 46.

September 17: Ven. Fulton J. Sheen, *Life of Christ* (New York: Image Books, 2008), 580.

September 18: St. John Henry Newman, *Prayers Before the Eucharist* (Charlotte, NC: TAN Books, 2019), 120.

September 19: Pope St. John Paul II, *Jesus, Son and Savior, A Catechesis on the Creed* (New York: Pauline Books & Media, 1989), 441.

September 20: St. Leo the Great, *The Liturgy of the Hours*, Vol. II (New York: Catholic Book Publishing Co., 1976), 313.

September 21: St. Matthew 27: 45–46, *Divine Mercy Catholic Bible, Revised Standard Version, Second Catholic Edition* (West Chester, PA: Ascension Publishing, 2001), 1309–1310.

September 22: St. Thomas of Villanova, *The Works of Saint Thomas of Villanova*, trans. by Daniel Hobbins and Matthew J. O'Connell (Villanova, PA: Augustinian Press, 2001), 178.

REFERENCES

September 23: St. Padre Pio, as quoted in *Padre Pio's Words of Hope*, Edited by Eileen Dunn Bertanzetti (Huntington, IN: Our Sunday Visitor, 1999), 39.

September 24: St. Paul of the Cross, *A Though For Every Day, On the Occasion of the 150ᵗʰ Anniversary of the Canonization of St. Paul of the Cross* (Rome: Convento dei PP Passionisti, 2017), 11.

September 25: G.K. Chesterton, *The Everyman Chesterton*, ed. by Ian Ker (London: Everyman's Library, 2011), 439.

September 26: St. John Vianney, The *Sermons of the Curé D'Ars*, trans. by Una Morrissy (Charlotte, NC: TAN Books, 1995), 181–182.

September 27: St. Vincent de Paul, as quoted in *Cultivating the Virtues, Self-Mastery With The Saints* (Charlotte, NC: TAN Books, 2016), 140.

September 28: St. Ignatius of Loyola, as quoted in *Cultivating the Virtues, Self-Mastery With The Saints* (Charlotte, NC: TAN Books, 2016), 142.

September 29: St. Padre Pio, as quoted in Gianluigi Pasquale, *Padre Pio's Spiritual Direction For Every Day*, trans. by Marsha Daigle-Williamson (Cincinnati, OH: Servant, 2011), 34.

September 30: St. Claude De La Colombière, *The Spiritual Direction of Saint Claude De La Colombière*, trans. by Mother M. Philip, I.B.V.M (San Francisco, CA: Ignatius Press, 2018), 74–75.

October Image: Bassetti Marcantonio (1586–1630). "Deposition of Christ" Public Domain.

October 1: St. Thérèse of Lisieux, *The Story of a Soul*, trans. by John Beevers (New York: Image, 2001), 160.

October 2: St. John Chrysostom, *The Liturgy of the Hours*, Vol. II (New York: Catholic Book Publishing Co., 1976), 473.

October 3: Ven. Fulton J. Sheen, *Life of Christ* (New York: Image Books, 2008), 518–519.

October 4: St. Francis of Assis, as quoted in St. Bonaventure, *The Life of St. Francis of Assisi* (Charlotte, NC: TAN Books, 1988), 132.

October 5: St. Faustina Kowalska, *Diary: Divine Mercy in My Soul* (Stockbridge, MA: Marian Press, 2005), no. 72.

October 6: St. Bruno, as quoted in *Saint Bruno The Carthusian* by Andre Ravier, S.J., trans. by Bruno Becker, O.S.B (San Francisco, CA: Ignatius Press, 1995), 177.

October 7: Ven. Mary of Ágreda, *The Mystical City of God*. Vol. III, trans. by Rev. George J. Blatter (Charlotte, NC: TAN Books, 2006), no. 554.

October 8: St. John Vianney, *The Sermons of the Curé D'Ars*, trans. by Una Morrissy (Charlotte, NC: TAN Books, 1995), 175.

October 9: St. John Henry Newman, *Prayers Before the Eucharist* (Charlotte, NC: TAN Books, 2019), 29.

October 10: St. Padre Pio, as quoted in Gianluigi Pasquale, *Padre Pio's Spiritual Direction For Every Day,* trans. by Marsha Daigle-Williamson (Cincinnati, OH: Servant, 2011), 39.

October 11: Pope St. John XXIII, *Journey of a Soul, the Autobiography of Pope John XXIII* (New York: Image Books, 1980), 368.

October 12: St. Stanislaus Papczyński, *Selected Writings*, trans. by Casimir Krzyzanowski, MIC, Patrick Lynch, MIC, Thaddaeus Lancton, MIC, and J.R. Thomas Holland (Stockbridge, MA: Marian Heritage, 2022), 422.

October 13: St. Louis De Montfort, *The Secret of the Rosary*, trans. Mary Barbour, T.O.P. (Bay Shore, NY: Montfort Publications, 2013), 131.

October 14: *The Catechism of the Council of Trent*, trans. by John A. McHugh, O.P. and Charles J Callan, O.P. (Charlotte, NC: TAN Books, 1982), 63.

October 15: St. Teresa of Ávila, as quoted in *Cultivating the Virtues, Self-Mastery With The Saints* (Charlotte, NC: TAN Books, 2016), 166.

October 16: St. Margaret Mary Alacoque, as quoted in *Devotion To The Sacred Heart* by Servant of God Fr. Lukas Etlin, O.S.B (Charlotte, NC: TAN Books, 2012). 17.

October 17: St. Ignatius of Antioch, *The Liturgy of the Hours*, Vol. IV (New York: Catholic Book Publishing Co., 1976), 1491.

October 18: St. Luke 23: 32–34, *Divine Mercy Catholic Bible, Revised Standard Version, Second Catholic Edition* (West Chester, PA: Ascension Publishing, 2001), 1384.

October 19: St. John De Brébeuf, *The Liturgy of the Hours*, Vol. IV (New York: Catholic Book Publishing Co., 1976), 1503.

October 20: St. Paul of the Cross, *The Liturgy of the Hours*, Vol. IV (New York: Catholic Book Publishing Co., 1976), 1505.

October 21: Ven. Fulton J. Sheen, *Life of Christ* (New York: Doubleday, 1977), 374.

October 22: Pope St. John Paul II, *Dives in Misericordia*, 7.

October 23: St. Paul of the Cross, *A Though For Every Day, On the Occasion of the 150ᵗʰ Anniversary of the Canonization of St. Paul of the Cross* (Romoe: Convento dei PP Passionisti, 2017), 11.

October 24: St. Anthony Mary Claret, *Autobiography* (Chicago, IL: Claretian Publications, 1976), 138–139.

October 25: St. Leo the Great, *The Liturgy of the Hours*, Vol. II (New York: Catholic Book Publishing Co., 1976), 313.

October 26: St. John Vianney, The *Sermons of the Curé D'Ars*, trans. by Una Morrissy (Charlotte, NC: TAN Books, 1995), 176.

October 27: St. Thomas Aquinas, as quoted in *Manual for Spiritual Warfare* (Charlotte, NC: TAN Books, 2014), 289.

October 28: Matthew 26: 52–54, *Divine Mercy Catholic Bible, Revised Standard Version, Second Catholic Edition* (West Chester, PA: Ascension Publishing, 2001), 1307.

October 29: St. Catherine of Siena, *The Liturgy of the Hours*, Vol. II (New York:. Catholic Book Publishing Co., 1976), 1794.

October 30: St. Claude De La Colombière, *The Spiritual Direction of Saint Claude De La Colombière,* trans. by Mother M. Philip, I.B.V.M (San Francisco, CA: Ignatius Press, 2018), 44.

October 31: St. John Chrysostom, as quoted in *Manual for Spiritual Warfare* (Charlotte, NC: TAN Books, 2014), 127.

November Image: Cresti Domenico Called Passignano (1559–1638). "Entombment of Christ". Public Domain.

November 1: Revelation 5: 9–10, 12, *Divine Mercy Catholic Bible, Revised Standard Version, Second Catholic Edition* (West Chester, PA: Ascension Publishing, 2001), 1589.

November 2: Mark 15: 2–5, *Divine Mercy Catholic Bible, Revised Standard Version, Second Catholic Edition* (West Chester, PA: Ascension Publishing, 2001), 1336–1337.

November 3: Bl. Anne Catherine Emmerich, *The Dolorous Passion of Our Lord Jesus Christ* (Charlotte, NC: TAN Books, 2004), 287.

November 4: Bl. Michael Sopoćko, *The Mercy of God in His Works*, trans. by B. Batchelor (Stockbridge, MA: Marian Fathers, 1962), 203.

November 5: Pope St. John Paul II, *On the Christian Meaning of Human Suffering*, 75.

November 6: Matthew 26: 55–56, *Divine Mercy Catholic Bible, Revised Standard Version, Second Catholic Edition* (West Chester, PA: Ascension Publishing, 2001), 1307.

November 7: St. Claude De La Colombière, *The Spiritual Direction of Saint Claude De La Colombière*, trans. by Mother M. Philip, I.B.V.M (San Francisco, CA: Ignatius Press, 2018), 75.

November 8: Bl. Elizabeth of the Trinity, *I Have Found God, Complete Works, Elizabeth of the Trinity, Letters from Carmel, Volume Two,* trans. by Anne Englund Nash (Washington, DC: ISC Publications, 1995), 263.

November 9: St. Paul of the Cross, *A Though For Every Day, On the Occasion of the 150ᵗʰ Anniversary of the Canonization of St. Paul of the Cross* (Rome: Convento dei PP Passionisti, 2017), 12.

November 10: St. Leo the Great, *The Liturgy of the Hours*, Vol. II (New York: Catholic Book Publishing Co., 1976), 1756.

November 11: St. John Chrysostom, *The Liturgy of the Hours,* Vol. II (New York: Catholic Book Publishing Co., 1976), 475.

November 12: St. Ambrose, *The Liturgy of the Hours*, Vol. II (New York: Catholic Book Publishing Co., 1976), 204.

November 13: Servant of God Luis Martinez, *Only Jesus,* trans. by Sr. Mary St. Daniel, BVM (London: B. Herder Book Co., 1962), 143.

November 14: St. Faustina Kowalska, *Diary: Divine Mercy in My Soul* (Stockbridge, MA: Marian Press, 2005), no. 1211.

November 15: Thomas à Kempis, *The Imitation of Christ,* trans. by Ronald Knox (San Francisco, CA: Ignatius Press, 2005), bk. 2, no. 12, 99.

November 16: St. Gertrude, as quoted in *Cultivating the Virtues, Self-Mastery With The Saints* (Charlotte, NC: TAN Books, 2016), 136.

November 17: 1 Peter 4: 12–14, *Divine Mercy Catholic Bible, Revised Standard Version, Second Catholic Edition* (West Chester, PA: Ascension Publishing, 2001), 1569.

November 18: St. Francis De Sales, *Roses Among Thorns* (Manchester, NH: Sophia Institute Press, 2014), 86.

REFERENCES

November 19: St. John Henry Newman, *Meditations & Devotions* (Brewster, MA: Paraclete Press, 2019), 55.

November 20: Ven. Mary of Ágreda, *The Mystical City of God*. Vol. III, trans. by Rev. George J. Blatter (Charlotte, NC: TAN Books, 2006), no. 671.

November 21: Ven. Fulton J. Sheen, *The World's First Love* (San Francisco, CA: Ignatius Press, 2011), 262.

November 22: St. Paul of the Cross, *A Though For Every Day, On the Occasion of the 150ᵗʰ Anniversary of the Canonization of St. Paul of the Cross* (Rome: Convento dei PP Passionisti, 2017), 13.

November 23: Luke 23: 35–38, *Divine Mercy Catholic Bible, Revised Standard Version, Second Catholic Edition* (West Chester, PA: Ascension Publishing, 2001), 1384.

November 24: Ven. Fulton J. Sheen, *Life of Christ* (New York: Doubleday, 1977), 388.

November 25: Bl. Jerzy Popiełuszko, as quoted in Bernard Brien, *Truth versus Totalitarianism* (San Francisco, CA: Ignatius Press, 2018), 72–73.

November 26: St. Louis De Montfort, *The Secret of the Rosary*, trans. Mary Barbour, T.O.P. (Bay Shore, NY: Montfort Publications, 2013), 76.

November 27: St. Augustine of Hippo, as quoted in *Cultivating the Virtues, Self-Mastery With The Saints* (Charlotte, NC: TAN Books, 2016), 132.

November 28: Bl. Anne Catherine Emmerich, *The Dolorous Passion of Our Lord Jesus Christ* (Charlotte, NC: TAN Books, 2004), 235.

November 29: Philippians 2:5–11, *Divine Mercy Catholic Bible, Revised Standard Version, Second Catholic Edition* (West Chester, PA: Ascension Publishing, 2001), 1521.

November 30: St. Anthony Mary Claret, as quoted in Donald H. Calloway, MIC, *Eucharistic Gems: Daily Wisdom on the Blessed Sacrament* (Stockbridge, MA: Marian Press, 2023), 17.

December Image: Albrecht Dürer (1471–1528). "The Holy Trinity". Public Domain.

December 1: St. Charles de Foucauld, as quoted in Jean-Jacques Antier, *Charles De Foucauld* (San Francisco, CA: Ignatius Press, 1999), 208.

December 2: St. Anthony of Padua, as quoted in Sophronius Clasen, O.F.M., *Saint Anthony Doctor of the Church* (Chicago, IL: Franciscan Herald Press, 1960), 43.

December 3: St. Francis Xavier, as quoted in *Cultivating the Virtues, Self-Mastery With The Saints* (Charlotte, NC: TAN Books, 2016), 147.

December 4: John 19: 9–11, *Divine Mercy Catholic Bible, Revised Standard Version, Second Catholic Edition* (West Chester, PA: Ascension Publishing, 2001), 1418.

December 5: St. Faustina Kowalska, *Diary: Divine Mercy in My Soul* (Stockbridge, MA: Marian Press, 2005), no. 1320.

December 6: St. Irenaeus, as quoted in *Manual for Spiritual Warfare* (Charlotte, NC: TAN Books, 2014), 126.

December 7: St. Ambrose, as quoted in St. Alphonsus de Liguori, *Dignity and Duties of the Priest* (Brooklyn, NY: Redemptorist Fathers, 1927), 388.

December 8: Bl. Pope Pius IX, *Ineffabilis Deus.*

December 9: St. Ephrem, *The Liturgy of the Hours*, Vol. II (New York: Catholic Book Publishing Co., 1976), 1869.

December 10: Luke 23: 8–12, *Divine Mercy Catholic Bible, Revised Standard Version, Second Catholic Edition* (West Chester, PA: Ascension Publishing, 2001), 1383–1384.

December 11: St. Ignatius of Loyola, *The Spiritual Exercises of Saint Ignatius* (Charlotte, NC: TAN Books, 1999), 161.

December 12: Ven. Mary of Ágreda, *The Mystical City of God*. Vol. III, trans. Rev. George J. Blatter (Charlotte, NC: TAN Books, 2006), no. 584.

December 13: St. Gregory the Great, *The Liturgy of the Hours*, Vol. II (New York: Catholic Book Publishing Co., 1976), 258.

December 14: St. John of the Cross, as quoted in *A Radical Love, Wisdom from Dorothy Day*, Edited by Patricia Mitchell (Ijamsville, MD: The Word Among Us, 2000), 132.

December 15: St. Louis De Montfort, *The Secret of the Rosary*, trans. Mary Barbour, T.O.P. (Bay Shore, NY: Montfort Publications, 2013), 78.

December 16: Ven. Fulton J. Sheen, *Life of Christ* (New York: Doubleday, 1977), 394.

December 17: Mark 14: 55–59, *Divine Mercy Catholic Bible, Revised Standard Version, Second Catholic Edition* (West Chester, PA: Ascension Publishing, 2001), 1335–1336.

December 18: G.K. Chesterton, *The Everyman Chesterton*, ed. by Ian Ker (London: Everyman's Library, 2011), 442–443.

REFERENCES

December 19: St. Paul of the Cross, *A Though For Every Day, On the Occasion of the 150ᵗʰ Anniversary of the Canonization of St. Paul of the Cross* (Rome: Convento dei PP Passionisti, 2017), 13.

December 20: Ven. Fulton J. Sheen, *Life of Christ* (New York: Image Books, 2008), 579.

December 21: St. Josemaría Escrivá, *Christ is Passing By* (New Rochelle, NY: Little Hills Press, 1990), 137.

December 22: Bl. Solanus Casey, as quoted in Br. Leo Wollenweber, O.F.M. Cap., *Meet Solanus Casey* (Cincinnati, OH: St. Anthony Messenger Press, 2002), 126.

December 23: St. John Henry Newman, *Meditations & Devotions* (Brewster, MA: Paraclete Press, 2019), 71.

December 24: St. Leo the Great, *The Liturgy of the Hours*, Vol. II (New York: Catholic Book Publishing Co., 1976), 359.

December 25: Ven. Fulton J. Sheen, *Life of Christ* (New York: Image Books, 2008), 539.

December 26: St. Stephen, first martyr, as quoted in Acts of the Apostles 7: 51–53, *Divine Mercy Catholic Bible, Revised Standard Version, Second Catholic Edition* (West Chester, PA: Ascension Publishing, 2001), 1432.

December 27: St. John 19: 33–35, *Divine Mercy Catholic Bible, Revised Standard Version, Second Catholic Edition* (West Chester, PA: Ascension Publishing, 2001), 1419.

December 28: St. Faustina Kowalska, *Diary: Divine Mercy in My Soul* (Stockbridge, MA: Marian Press, 2005), no. 1512.

December 29: St. Augustine of Hippo, *The Liturgy of the Hours*, Vol. II (New York: Catholic Book Publishing Co., 1976), 169.

December 30: Pope St. John Paul II, *Jesus, Son and Savior, A Catechesis on the Creed* (New York: Pauline Books & Media, 1989), 439.

December 31: St. Maximilian Kolbe, *Stronger Than Hatred, A Collection of Spiritual Writings*, trans. by Edward Flood (New York: New City Press, 1988), 101.

About the Author

Father Donald Calloway, MIC, a convert to Catholicism, is a member of the Congregation of Marian Fathers of the Immaculate Conception. Before his conversion to Catholicism, he was a high school dropout who had been kicked out of a foreign country, institutionalized twice, and thrown in jail multiple times.

After his radical conversion, he earned a B.A. in Philosophy and Theology from the Franciscan University of Steubenville, Ohio; M.Div. and S.T.B. degrees from the Dominican House of Studies in Washington, D.C.; and an S.T.L. in Mariology from the International Marian Research Institute in Dayton, Ohio.

He is the author of 20 books, including the international bestseller *Consecration to St. Joseph: The Wonders of Our Spiritual Father* (Marian Press, 2020) that has been translated into more than 25 languages. He currently serves as the Vicar Provincial and Vocation Director for the Mother of Mercy Province.

Father Calloway leads pilgrimages to Marian Shrines around the world. Find out more at FatherCalloway.com

To learn more about Marian vocations, visit
Marian.org/vocations

or visit Fr. Calloway's website,
FatherCalloway.com

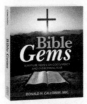

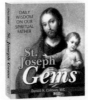

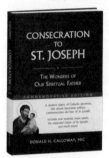
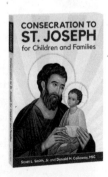

More Inspiration from Fr. Calloway

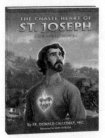

THE CHASTE HEART OF ST. JOSEPH
A GRAPHIC NOVEL

How much do you really know about St. Joseph? He was once a little boy and played like all children. He had royal blood, and could have been a king. He was a young man when he married Mary. He was a wonderful father to Jesus. He was the brave and steadfast protector of the Holy Family. He's the model of manhood. He's worked many miracles and is a powerful intercessor for us … And he had a pure, chaste heart. Join Fr. Calloway as he tells the dynamic and inspiring story of St. Joseph, our spiritual father and the "Terror of Demons." You'll learn that, whenever you need help, just "Go to Joseph!" Hardcover. 84 pages. Y123-JOEG

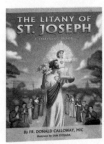

THE LITANY OF ST. JOSEPH
COLORING BOOK

Color, learn, pray! Father Donald Calloway, MIC, presents a fun way for children of all ages to grow closer to St. Joseph, the ultimate superhero and the "Terror of Demons." Learn more about this great Saint by coloring the wonderful illustrations by Sam Estrada, each portraying a different title of St. Joseph. 36 pages. Y123-JCOBK

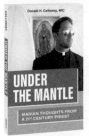

UNDER THE MANTLE
MARIAN THOUGHTS FROM A 21ST CENTURY PRIEST

Father Calloway deftly shares his personal insights on topics including the Eucharist, the papacy, the Church, Confession, Divine Mercy, prayer, the Cross, masculinity, and femininity. The Blessed Virgin Mary is the central thread weaving a tapestry throughout with quotes about Our Lady from saints, blesseds, and popes. Paperback. 300 pages. Y123-UTM 🅔

Call 1-800-462-7426 or visit FatherCalloway.com

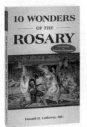

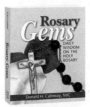

The Marian Fathers of Today and Tomorrow

What are you looking for in the priests of tomorrow?

- ☑ Zeal for proclaiming the Gospel
- ☑ Faithfulness to the Pope and Church teaching
- ☑ Love of Mary Immaculate
- ☑ Love of the Holy Eucharist
- ☑ Concern for the souls in Purgatory
- ☑ Dedication to bringing God's mercy to all souls

These are the top reasons why men pursuing a priestly vocation are attracted to the Congregation of Marian Fathers of the Immaculate Conception.

Please support the education of these future priests. More than 30 Marian seminarians are counting on your gift.

Call: 1-800-462-7426
Online: Marian.org/helpseminarians

Join the
Association of Marian Helpers,
headquartered at the
National Shrine of The Divine Mercy,
and share in special blessings!

**An invitation from
Fr. Joseph, MIC, the director**

**Marian Helpers is an Association of Christian faithful of the
Congregation of Marians of the Immaculate Conception.**

By becoming a member, you share in the spiritual benefits
of the daily Masses, prayers, and good works of the
Marian priests and brothers.

This is a special offer of grace given to you by the Church
through the Marian Fathers. Please consider this opportunity
to share in these blessings, along with others whom you
would wish to join into this spiritual communion.

The Marian Fathers of the Immaculate Conception of the
Blessed Virgin Mary is a religious congregation of nearly 500
priests and brothers around the world.

Call 1-800-462-7426 or visit Marian.org